~ DR. ADAM ELMEGIRAB'S ~

BOOK OF BITTERS

~ DR. ADAM ELMEGIRAB'S ~
BOOK OF BITTERS

THE BITTER AND TWISTED HISTORY OF ONE OF THE COCKTAIL WORLD'S MOST FASCINATING INGREDIENTS

DOG 'N' BONE

Published in 2017 by Dog 'n' Bone Books
An imprint of Ryland Peters & Small Ltd

20–21 Jockey's Fields   341 E 116th St
London WC1R 4BW   New York, NY 10029

www.rylandpeters.com

10 9 8 7 6 5 4 3 2 1

A CIP catalog record for this book is available from the
Library of Congress and the British Library.

ISBN: 978 1 909313 94 1

Printed in China

Editor: Nathan Joyce
Design and illustration: Abigail Read
Photographer: Terry Benson
Stylist: Kim Sullivan

Additional image credits: p8 taken from *The Bon Vivant's
Companion or How to Mix Drinks* by "Professor" Jerry Thomas,
1862; p12 Getty Images/De Agostini Picture Library/
Contributor; p15 Getty Images/De Agostini Picture Library/
Biblioteca Ambrosiana; p20 Getty Images/Buyenlarge/
Contributor; p22 Getty Images/GraphicaArtis/Contributor;
p23 Bob's Bitters; p24 The Bitter Truth; p25 Dr. Adam
Elmegirab's Bitters; p27 Getty Images/ilbusca; p31 Getty
Images/Mashuk; p33 Getty Images/Duncan1890; p123
Callooh Callay Bar

CONTENTS

1.
THE BEGINNING OF BITTERS

Introduction 8

Defining Bitters 10
The Origin of Bitters 12
Bitter Ain't Bad 14

The Cock-tail 15
The Angostura Myth 16

2.
BITTERS DECONSTRUCTED

The Rise and Fall of Bitters 20
The Rebirth of Bitters 23
The Bitters Manufacturing
    Process 26

3.
UNDERSTANDING BITTERNESS

The Science of Taste and Flavor   36
Botanical Overview 40
Bittering Agents 41
Selecting and Pairing Bitters 48

4.
COCKTAILS

Bartending Equipment 52
Glassware 54
Techniques 55
A Note on Recipes 57

The Drinks

Bitter 58
Sweet 86
Salt 104
Sour 114
Umami 132

Key Ingredient Recipes 150
Bitters Glossary 156

INDEX
158

ACKNOWLEDGMENTS
160

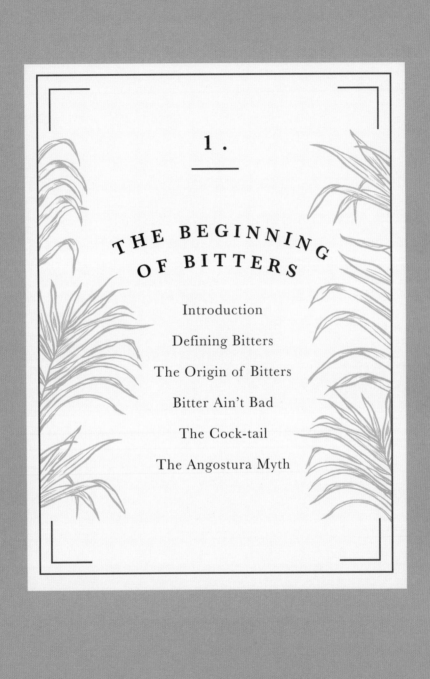

1.

THE BEGINNING OF BITTERS

Introduction

Defining Bitters

The Origin of Bitters

Bitter Ain't Bad

The Cock-tail

The Angostura Myth

INTRODUCTION

———

The Bon Vivant's Companion or How to Mix Drinks, written by "Professor" Jerry Thomas in 1862, is the holy grail for bartenders and recognized as the first cocktail book ever published. To this day, cocktail aficionados and bartenders seek out original copies from auction sites, book stores, and vintage markets in the faint hope of finding a relatively inexpensive copy. First editions of Thomas's work change hands for hundreds if not thousands of pounds, so most are happy to settle for a cheaper modern reprint.

Housing a collection of drink styles, the tome gives over 200 mixed-drink recipes for punches, egg nogs, cocktails, juleps, smashes, cobblers, crustas, mulls, sangarees, toddies, slings, shrubs, and flips, many of which are still made to this day, both in their original form or as the basis for a modern adaptation. These recipes, all predating Thomas and going as far back as the 16th and 17th centuries, are essentially the building blocks for any aspiring bartender or drink enthusiast who wishes to immerse themselves in the world of mixed drinks. Much in the same way that chefs will learn the five mother sauces, bartenders should get to grips with these families of drinks as a fundamental undertaking in becoming a professional bartender.

Through my years of working behind bars during the rebirth of cocktail culture, having started bartending in late 2001, *The Bon Vivant's Companion* was never far from reach, regularly providing insight and inspiration when creating new drinks and designing cocktail menus. My passion for all things cocktail began to extend into collecting old spirits and liqueurs, which people typically hoard away for investment, though I would open every bottle I purchased for the simple reason that I wanted to know how things used to taste. Noting clear differences between the products of yesteryear compared to those produced nowadays, primarily due to the degradation/oxygenation of older products coupled with improvements in production techniques, I started to question why we would recreate old recipes as originally detailed when much had changed. Sugar wasn't as refined, citrus wouldn't have been as fresh since food tranportation took longer in the past, and even eggs were smaller a century ago compared to what we find on store shelves today. This didn't sit right with me, nor my analytical viewpoint on life, so I set out to research things further.

In 2007 I started a blog page titled the *Jerry Thomas Project*—quite simply a venture to recreate all the drinks from Thomas's bartender's guide as he would have made them, using the old spirits and ingredients I'd collected, and comparing them to how we make them now with modern ingredients and drink-making techniques. The blog proved to be a huge success, gaining a following of readers from around the world, but things really escalated when I started planning ahead to try and obtain a bottle of the Bogart's Bitters which Thomas detailed in a number of recipes. I would quickly learn that there was never any such thing as Bogart's Bitters, this was actually a typesetter's error corrected in later editions of Thomas's book. The ingredient which should have been referenced was in fact *Boker's* Bitters. Originally imported into the United States in 1828 by Düsseldorf immigrant Johann Gottlieb Böker, the company closed in the 1920s following the ravages of the Pure Food & Drug Act and the Volstead Act (the latter commonly referred to as Prohibition), which put paid to the company. More on that later.

If an original copy of *The Bon Vivant's Companion* is the bartending holy grail, finding a bottle of Boker's Bitters is like finding life on another planet—it is extremely sought-after in the bottle-collecting community due to the rare Lady's Leg style of bottle in which the liquid was housed. It makes me shudder knowing the contents, which are so highly prized by the bar community, are considered an afterthought and have been disposed of by some bottle collectors. Knowing Boker's were extremely rare and wouldn't be easy to come by, I set about recreating my own approximation. This involved a four-fold process: (i) submitting old samples to a lab for GC/MS analysis (Gas Chromatography/Mass Spectrometry); (ii) contacting descendants of the previous owners of the Boker's Bitters brand to ascertain if an original recipe still existed within the families; (iii) comparing recipes for counterfeit Boker's which appeared in books and pharmaceutical guides from the 1800s to find a common theme with the ingredients while correlating this data with analysis conducted on Boker's by the temperance movement; (iv) and studying old court records in cases where the owners of the Boker's Bitters company had started legal proceedings against producers of counterfeit bottlings, primarily to determine if any crucial information was shared in the testimonies. While no original recipe would show up, with my search ongoing I would gain a wealth of information from my 18 months of research, crucially identifying specific details as to the ingredients used

in the original formulation. Having carried out the most in-depth research on the Boker's Bitters brand I was left with more than enough to create an excellent reformulation that would be mindful of its predecessor, but also work perfectly in modern drinks.

My first batch would consist of five bottlings, decanted into used Angostura Orange Bitters bottles. The label was designed by my good friend Christian Bell, not too dissimilar to the label that adorns bottles of my Boker's today. In 2009, after I shared my research on my blog along with a photo of the bottles, I thought that would be the end of it and people would wait to hear about how they worked in the original drinks, but it was only the beginning. Within a week I'd received the best part of 1,000 enquiries from bartenders all around the world who wanted to buy a bottle for themselves. The *Jerry Thomas Project* was never intended to be a moneymaking exercise but the costs involved, along with the additional time and effort spent reformulating Boker's, meant that this opportunity to make some money back was too good to turn down. The plan was to produce 1,000 bottles of the new Boker's Bitters, sell them on a first come, first served basis, then get back to completing the *Jerry Thomas Project*. What actually happened was the birth of Dr. Adam Elmegirab's Bitters Ltd. in 2009, with the Doctor branding being a tongue-in-cheek nod to the original medicinal use of bitters. In time, I would have six different products on the market, four collaborations with world-famous bars and brands, exports to over 30 countries worldwide, and a passport full of stamps. I've now had the best part of a decade immersing myself in the history of bitters. This is their story…

———

Figure 1. (opposite) Jerry Thomas
Figure 2. (right) A bottle of Boker's Bitters

DEFINING BITTERS

———

"What exactly are bitters?" is one of the most common questions I've been asked over the years and I've found no better definition than that found in *The Standard Manual of Soda and Other Beverages: A Treatise Especially Adapted to the Requirements of Druggists and Confectioners,* first published in 1897:

"BITTERS. - These are made by extracting bitter and aromatic—or bitter only— drugs with a mixture of alcohol and water; sometimes a small amount of sugar or syrup is added."

At this point it should be acknowledged that bitters have evolved over the centuries into two key sub-categories. The first was historically used to improve the flavor of lesser-refined wines, gins, and brandies, acted as a hangover cure of sorts, and was the defining ingredient in the family of drinks known as the cock-tail. In their contemporary guise they're more closely associated with the culinary world and are widely used as a flavoring extract in food and beverages through brands such as Angostura, Peychaud's, The Bitter Truth, Bittermens, and Dr. Adam Elmegirab's. The bitters in the second sub-category have always been marketed as natural remedies and dominated the world of medicine in the 18th and 19th centuries before largely falling by the wayside in the early 20th century with the proliferation of pharmacies. They do still exist today, though, thanks to the likes of NatureWorks, Napier's, and Urban Moonshine, to name but a few practitioners of herbal bitters.

"BITTERS. — THESE ARE MADE BY EXTRACTING BITTER AND AROMATIC—OR BITTER ONLY— DRUGS WITH A MIXTURE OF ALCOHOL AND WATER; SOMETIMES A SMALL AMOUNT OF SUGAR OR SYRUP IS ADDED."

Though they have different marketing focuses, all the aforementioned brands stay true to using natural botanicals to obtain their desired flavor profiles with the bitter component being key to their botanical formula. The consumption of bitter plants and botanicals increases the production of saliva and digestive juices within the human body, an evolutionary advancement by way of the development of bitter taste receptors which assist the body in recognizing when toxic plants have been ingested. In modern times, the reliance on bitters as a medicinal aid is almost exclusively related to their use for their digestive properties, while also working as a remedy for heartburn and hiccups. Please note, and trust me on this, that is the only time I will happily extol the virtues of bitters as medicine. I've lost count of the number of guests I've *cured* over the years by offering up a glass of soda water with bitters when they were suffering after a heavy night or a large meal. Try it, it works.

The ongoing debate between pharmaceutical medicine versus natural remedies is long, complex, and better saved for the pages of another book, though both sides will undoubtedly agree that bitters are as good a digestive aid as any, especially so in modern diets such as those found in the USA, which is almost sugar-philic and bitter-phobic. In stark contrast to the diet of European countries such as Italy and France who embrace bitterness like no other. Simply compare typical coffee serves in those countries and it will tell you all you need to know.

With all that said, bitters are now predominantly used as a flavoring, with the bitter element arguably an after-thought, so their definition has loosened somewhat and the term has, rightly or wrongly, become all-encapsulating. Classicists such as myself (like those who maintain that London Dry Gin should have a dominant flavor of juniper) will always support the stance that a true bitters should have an inherently bitter backbone provided by a bittering agent—the bittering agent being the bitter "drug" as referenced in the *Standard Manual* definition. Those are most commonly roots and barks with proven medicinal qualities, such as gentian root, cinchona bark, quassia bark, and dandelion root, but also plant life such as wormwood and hops, each recognizable by their usage in a wide variety of beverages, including fortified wines, tonic water, beers, sodas, and gin. Tinctures are extracts which focus on a single botanical and often get tagged with the bitters moniker, but they are really a category in their own right, and extracts made with synthetic flavorings, or those built on a base of glycerin in place of alcohol, have found a place in the armory of chefs and bartenders, even if they are not a bitters in the truest sense of the word.

The aromatic drug also described by the *Standard Manual* is exactly that, botanicals with an aromatic and flavorful profile. These include citrus peels, fruits, herbs, flowers, and spices, which either work in harmony to accentuate and complement a dominant flavor such as the orange in an Orange Bitters, or in combination to form a classic style of aromatic bitters such as Angostura, Peychaud's, Amargo Chuncho, Boker's, or Underberg, which bring a wide variety of flavor to the forefront and don't necessarily have a central focal point. On the face of it, bitters are a relatively simple concoction to understand but their history, production processes, and usage are anything but.

Figure 3. (above)
i Star anise
ii Cinchona bark
iii Angelica
iv Orange peel
v Wormwood

The histories of alcohol and medicine are long intertwined with almost all alcoholic products, including whisk(e)y, wine, vodka, gin, vermouth, beer, and in this case bitters, having been created and consumed for their alleged medicinal benefits and perceived health-giving properties. Excavations of Skara Brae in the Orkney Islands, a Neolithic settlement that was occupied from around 3180BC to 2500BC, uncovered large pottery jars which contained the remnants of an alcoholic beverage produced from oats and barley and flavored with meadowsweet, as well as poisonous nightshade, hemlock, and henbane. However, the oldest record of a medicinal alcoholic beverage dates even farther back to 7000BC in Jiahu, China, where a residue from a beverage produced

from rice, honey, grapes, and hawthorn fruits was discovered in 2004. Ancient Egyptians were also known to produce beer and wine, with residues of wine samples from Greece dating back to the same period of around 4000–3000BC. There is evidence of fermented horse's milk being consumed by the Mongols, mead (*aka honey wine*) by the Celts, and pulque from corn produced by the Mayans. As long as humans have roamed the earth we've consumed alcohol for medicinal reasons, likely discovered accidentally by eating fermented fruit. *"Let's drink to health"* is one of the oldest toasts in existence and it's easy to understand why.

Adding natural botanicals, such as herbs, spices, roots, and barks, to alcohol created a more effective form of medicine due to the fact that the ethanol in alcohol is a powerful solvent which dissolves many organic compounds, but also acts as a means to preserve botanical matter. It is this combination of alcohol and botanicals that gave rise to the likes of vermouth, gin, and bitters. The father of modern medicine, the Greek physician Hippocrates, was famed for serving his patients a wormwood wine infused with herbs and spices. This wormwood wine can easily be viewed as an early form of vermouth, which of course derives its name from the German word *"wermut,"* meaning wormwood.

While vermouth must contain wormwood to be classified as vermouth, bitters are not too dissimilar, being a more concentrated variant primarily relying on a spiritous base constructed with a variety of bittering agents. Their emergence and popularity is often lazily credited to Johann Gottlieb Benjamin Siegert of Angostura Bitters fame but they'd been around long before his time. The second man typically credited with creating bitters is the London apothecary Richard Stoughton with his Elixir Magnum Stomachium of 1690, also referred to as the Great Cordial Elixir. I believe the confusion stems from the fact his bitters received a royal patent in 1712, the second medicine to be granted one, although there's no disputing Stoughton's marketing skills and his involvement in popularizing bitters. As drinks historian Dave Wondrich detailed to me, *"His ads were everywhere, in all the sporting literature of the day, and he pushed his bitters as tasting good which was very important."* On top of that, he targeted his bitters as a cure for hangovers and digestive issues, two common ailments of the period, which was an unquestionable factor in his success throughout the 18th century. Despite Stoughton's role in the history of bitters he had actually followed in the footsteps of Thomas Sydenham, the true father of bitters and one of the first to champion the use of Peruvian bark, the source of quinine.

Unlike most bitters, whose primary focus was to treat ailments related to the stomach and digestion, Sydenham's Bitters were created as a cure for gout, a form of inflammatory arthritis that attacks the joints, commonly at the base of the big toe. He wrote in his *Treatise on the Gout* (1683) that *"...gout generally attacks those aged persons, who have spent most of their lives in ease, voluptuousness, high living, and too free an use of wine and other spirituous liquors, and at length, by reason of the common inability to motion in old age, entirely left off those exercises, which young persons commonly use."* Sydenham came to be known as the "English Hippocrates," which is fitting as he clearly idolized Hippocrates and often referred to him in his works.

Sydenham lamented the traditional and often violent therapies of the time which included purging (*removing blood*) and emetics (which *induced vomiting*), instead recommending a gentler approach that consisted of a change in diet, regular exercise, a large intake of fluids—especially barley water which was also recommended by Hippocrates—and the consumption of his digestive medicine, Sydenham's Bitters. These were made from bitter botanicals such as angelica root, elfdock root, ground pine, wormwood leaves, and centaurium, as well as antiscorbutics (*medicines that counteract scurvy*) such as watercress and horseradish. These bitters proved to be a popular remedy for gout, probably because they were commonly consumed by adding them to Canary wine, a sweet white wine from

the Canary Islands that was extremely popular in Britain in the 17th century. Sydenham's teachings were significant in convincing many that the disease may be incurable and that the savage methods often deployed in treating it would actually aggravate the gout. Most importantly, his analytical approach developed a profile that sufferers could identify with, and the success of his bitters would see other medical practitioners attempt to imitate what Sydenham had created. With Sydenham's work the category of bitters was born...

Figure 4 . (opposite) Thomas Sydenham
Figure 5. (above) Apothecary bottles

BITTER AIN'T BAD

Before we even consider the taste of bitter and how it's generally perceived when consumed, one only needs to think of the language around it and the negative connotations it conveys. As an example, the following meanings can be found in the Oxford English dictionary under bitter: *"Having a sharp, pungent taste or smell,"* in relation to the taste of bitter foods; *"Feeling or showing anger, hurt, or resentment because of bad experiences or a sense of unjust treatment,"* if someone has bitter feelings; *"full of anger and acrimony,"* as could be felt after a bitter divorce battle; or *"intensely cold,"* as I often find in bitter Scottish winters. If someone is unhappy at work you could say they were *"embittered,"* and if you were finding it difficult to face up to the harsh reality of a situation you would be struggling to deal with the *"bitter truth."*

The negativity associated with bitter is understandable when you consider that humans have evolved a deep-seated distaste for bitterness, after all this reaction is the body's natural defence mechanism. An adverse reaction to bitterness is at its strongest in humans while we are very young, as smaller doses of poisons would be required to harm or kill us, but thankfully as we age the dislike of bitter tastes dulls. This explains why people generally grow to appreciate commonly bitter food and drink, such as coffee, beer, whisky, brandy, bittersweet/dark chocolate, and kale. This appreciation of bitter is heightened by the fact that we come to realize that bitter foods and drinks stimulate us, and in some cases are actually beneficial for our health in protecting against disease and illness. Bitter phytochemicals such as naringin (*found in grapefruit*), quercetin (*black olives and bittersweet/dark chocolate*), and epicatechin (*blackberries and green tea*) have all been shown to work as antioxidants, anti-inflammatories (to reduce prostate inflammation, for example), and to lower the risk of cancer. Research is still in its infancy and ongoing, but many medical professionals agree that bitter compounds have a positive effect on multiple bodily systems.

While our bodies may initially be telling us to avoid them, it seems the world is waking up to the joys of bitter tastes. Look at the growing interest in craft beer and the various bitter hops brewers use, coffees which have a wide spectrum of bitter tastes dependent on the level of roast, chocolate with a higher cacao content, and cocktails which regularly use a diverse selection of bitter liqueurs and spirits. Bitterness is essential to balance against sweetness, and I can't imagine there's a chef or bartender out there who would reject the use of bitter ingredients. They add depth and complexity, but most importantly they make things taste delicious.

Bitter, as with all tastes, is wholly subjective and is undoubtedly the most complex of our five tastes. Heat, color, and texture all play a vital role in how our bodies recognize tastes. The means by which we come to appreciate bitter tastes encapsulates a host of factors including our previous experiences (whether they be positive or negative), the culture we're surrounded by, and the society we grow up in. Consider the European way of life and diet, and the historical link to the forefathers of bitter medicine that will have been passed down through generations, which both perfectly lend themselves to a larger appreciation of bitter.
I'll raise a Negroni to that!

Figure 6. (above) The vermouth in a Martini adds bitterness and flavor
Figure 7. (opposite) A 19th-century cocktail bar scene

THE COCK-TAIL

———

In the 17th and 18th centuries, long before the word "cocktail" became a catch-all term for all beverages containing three or more ingredients, mixed drinks were widely recognized and grouped in families such as the sling (*spirit, sugar, water*), toddy (*spirit, sugar, hot water*), sour (*spirit, sugar, citrus*), or highball (*single spirit and carbonated mixer*). A cocktail, meanwhile, was defined by editor Harry Croswell in 1806, in response to a reader's question which asked: "What is a cocktail?" Croswell's answer was published in *The Balance and Columbian Repository* on May 13, 1806, and defined a cocktail as a style of drink in its own right:

"Cock-tail is a stimulating liquor, composed of spirits of any kind, sugar, water, and bitters—it is vulgarly called bittered sling, and is supposed to be an excellent electioneering potion, in as much as it renders the heart stout and bold, at the same time that it fuddles the head. It is said, also to be of great use to a democratic candidate: because a person, having swallowed a glass of it, is ready to swallow any thing else."

Simply put, the defining ingredient of a true cocktail is bitters, and the best example of a true cocktail is the Old Fashioned, which got its name from patrons in the latter part of the 1800s asking for a traditional "*Old Fashioned cocktail,*" in lieu of the jazzed up variants many bartenders were then offering.

BITTER AIN'T BAD

15

THE ANGOSTURA MYTH

Setting out on my career in the drinks industry in 2001, bitters quickly became commonplace in my life. As a young bartender keen to impress, I wanted to absorb as much information as I could about every bottle we sold on the bar; after all Sir Francis Bacon wasn't wrong when he wrote *"Knowledge is power."* When it came to researching the likes of vodka, rum, beer, wine, tequila, et al., it was relatively easy to access information on their history and production, especially with the proliferation of the Internet in the early 2000s. However, when asking questions about the little bottles of bitters with the oversized labels we were dashing in a large percentage of our cocktails, no one knew anything about them other than repeating the same fact, *"Angostura Bitters is poisonous"* or *"Angostura Bitters are used as rat poison."* This always seemed nonsensical to me, especially as it was a key ingredient in a wealth of cocktail recipes, doubly so after reading the label and ascertaining it was created by one Dr. J.G.B. Siegert. *"Why would a doctor create a poison that we still use in drinks almost 200 years later?"* I asked myself. It sounds even more absurd just writing that out. Professionally my interest was piqued...

Recreationally when my friends and I first started venturing out to bars, we would become regular drinkers of these allegedly poisonous bitters because they are key to the flavor profile of the infamous Scottish drink, the Long Vodka. The ritual behind its preparation even perpetuates the myth:

"Take one clean highball glass, dash in 2 or 3 drops of Angostura Bitters, roll the vessel between your hands to coat the glass before shaking off any excess bitters. To finish, fill your glass with ice, then add a shot of vodka, half that of lime cordial, and fill with lemonade."

The crucial element of this recipe is in ensuring only the merest hint of Angostura made it into the final drink because, as you were warned, *"You don't want to poison your guest."* The origins of the Long Vodka are largely unknown and it seems to be mostly consumed in Scotland, though it does sporadically have a cult following in random cities across the globe, and anyone who has been to Australia may well have heard of Lemon, Lime, & Bitters, essentially a Long Vodka *sans* alcohol which is an incredible refresher for hot days. The vodka will warm you when it's cold, and as Scotsmen we're naturally inclined to add a measure or two of vodka. I don't know what it says for Scottish drinking habits because even in the face of guests warning bartenders that Angostura Bitters were poisonous, they'd still happily part with their hard-earned cash to consume them en masse. So where did the myth that Angostura Bitters are poisonous originate, and why is the myth only really voiced in Europe? Let's go back 200 years to the time when bitter drugs were king.

Before we had modern pharmacies that primarily stock medicines in tablet or powder form, medicines were largely doled out in apothecaries, which sold a myriad of wines, spices, and herbs deemed to have medicinal value. This was also a time when almost anything bitter was believed to have medicinal properties. For example, consider the wormwood herb, gentian root, or cinchona bark (*the source of quinine*), just three famed bitter drugs of the period.

It's easy to understand why it was long a desire of medical experts to find cheaper alternative bitter plant extracts—the next big thing in the bitter drugs world if you must. Trinidadian doctors knew of one such drug, the bark of the *Cusparia febrifuga* plant, nowadays more commonly referred to as Angostura bark, which was widely used in the region to treat malaria. Through Catalonian monks who had settled in the area with the Spanish colonists in the 17th and 18th centuries, word of the bark and its alleged medicinal properties spread back to Europe and quickly gained traction with apothecaries across Central Europe. It is William Thomas Brande, the apothecary to Queen Consort Charlotte, who is credited with bringing wider knowledge of the bark, after he was alerted to a shipment which arrived in Great Britain in 1788. By 1797 some 44,000 lbs (20,000 kilos) had been exported to Europe.

In 1803, following the death of a child in Hamburg who had been given a decoction of Angostura bark, the city physician Johann Jakob Rambach was called in to investigate this new drug. Visiting several apothecaries and obtaining samples, he quickly ascertained that the decoction actually contained two different barks, leaving Rambach to conclude this second bark, hereinafter referred to as false Angostura, was poisonous and responsible for the child's passing. Rambach's early suspicions were that this false Angostura originated from the nux-vomica tree, a major source of strychnine. A highly poisonous and bitter alkaloid, strychnine is widely used today as a rodenticide, although at one time it was extensively used for its perceived medicinal qualities, namely as a stimulant and a remedy for heart problems.

More deaths would occur across Europe, leading authorities throughout the continent to take various levels of action. In Hamburg, they would sanction fines if apothecaries sold Angostura bark without approval. In Russia, residents were taught how to tell the difference between both barks; and in Austria authorities arranged for the destruction of all Angostura bark, true and false, while also banning its importation. Further investigations of European apothecaries led to the discovery that nearly all Angostura bark was contaminated with this second poisonous bark, though how this came to be led to much speculation. The origin of false Angostura was widely debated, but many accounts surfaced attributing it to, and ultimately agreeing that it originated from, India, where it was then shipped to England to be used as a febrifuge (*a medicine used to reduce fever*). Following a lack of sales, the cheaper false Angostura then made its way across to Holland where it was disposed of by mixing it with the highly popular true Angostura bark, thus contaminating samples. It was not until 1837 that Rambach's suspicions were proven and it was demonstrated that this false Angostura was indeed snakewood, the bark of the toxic nux-vomica tree (*Strychnos nux-vomica*).

Angostura Bitters have always maintained that their formula has never contained true Angostura bark, to the extent that they specifically detail it on the bottle. While this is most likely a response to distance themselves from the myth and the false Angostura bark scandal, it should be clarified that true Angostura bark is in no way poisonous and is to this day used to flavor food and drink, offering up a bitter mace-like taste and aroma. It is the association by name and through Chinese Whispers* over the last two centuries that have conspired to enhance the myth that Angostura Bitters are poisonous.

* *A game where one person whispers a message to another; this then continues down a line of people until the last player announces the message to the entire group, often leading to a very different result to the original message.*

2.

———

BITTERS DECONSTRUCTED

The Rise and Fall of Bitters

The Rebirth of Bitters

The Bitters
Manufacturing Process

THE RISE AND FALL OF BITTERS

With the rebirth of cocktail culture around the world, the bitters category has risen like a phoenix from the flames, having all but disappeared for the best part of a century, with only the likes of Angostura from Trinidad & Tobago, Peychaud's from Louisiana, Fee Brother's from New York, and Hermes from Tokyo carrying the torch throughout that time. Khoosh Bitters from Liverpool, UK, was popular with the British Empire in India but, strangely, it was never exported to the United States. Khoosh was around for the early part of the 20th century and was notably included in the *Café Royal Cocktail Book* (1937), but never gained the success of the aforementioned four. Despite their dominance in the 18th and 19th centuries the demise of bitters was swift and somewhat sudden, but their downfall was complex with a multitude of factors being responsible.

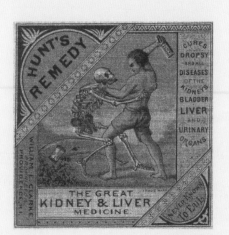

Following their birth in the late 17th century and subsequent growth throughout the 18th century, the 19th century would be the real heyday for bitters with hundreds of products on the open market, available over the counter without prescription. Originally a form of patent, or proprietary, medicine with many original examples having genuine medicinal qualities, the bitters category was saturated by a wealth of products that never got close to obtaining a patent but were nonetheless afforded government protection due to their trademarks. With the huge demand and lower taxation on bitters versus straight alcohol such as whisky, gin, or brandy, it's easy to understand why producing bitters was tempting for

many unscrupulous traders. The lack of regulation meant these quacks could formulate an alleged medicine and dress up its supposed effectiveness to an unsuspecting public, often with deadly consequences. Before modern medicine as we know it today, their cure-all claims were wild and elaborate, with everything from jaundice, diarrhea, colic, headaches, dysentery, and palpitations apparently curable by consuming their rogue concoctions.

Genuine bitters recipes predominantly originated in England, and later in Germany, receiving a level of gravitas after gaining grants to produce medicinal bitters for the British royal family. Bitters made their way over to the New World along with the first settlers from England, quickly gaining traction and becoming a huge industry that was promptly hijacked by the aforementioned unscrupulous traders. Their fraudulent sales and marketing approach could arguably be seen as genius: not disclosing the ingredients used in their bitters; claiming they were passed down from century-old folk recipes; aiming their advertising, which asserted the bitters to be beneficial to children, at desperate parents seeking to heal sick offspring; or targeting women and citing their products as a remedy for female discomforts.

Often these illicit bitters contained poisonous botanicals, and drugs such as opium or cocaine were widely used too, which caused addiction. Throughout the bitters boom, many medical professionals and physicians questioned the manufacturers' claims, highlighting the fact they did not cure what they alleged. They were supported by the temperance movement, which demanded total abstinence from alcohol. Beginning in the 1820s, the movement became larger and louder through the later part of the 19th century. However, while the movement succeeded in making drinking alcohol more socially unacceptable, it was unintentionally responsible for the growth of bitters consumption, which people claimed they were doing for medicinal purposes. As opposed to having a large pour of whiskey, you'd sip a large measure of alcoholic bitters instead. The movement, however, did do some good in ridding the world of unscrupulous dealers by repeatedly pointing out the alcoholic strength and apparent dangers of the botanical formulae of bitters in some of their propaganda booklets. As time progressed and scepticism surrounded the bitters industry, the American populace increasingly got on board, campaigning for laws to make producers divulge the contents of their bitters and tone down their purported advertising claims.

In 1881 the Proprietary Association was formed by a group of medical producers. It was created as a response to the temperance movement, the growing calls for full disclosure, and to protect many of the patented medicines on the market. The association's cause was supported by the written media principally because the press had grown somewhat dependent on the revenue provided by medical advertising in their newspapers and magazines. Unbelievably, some members of the print media did not only stay silent on the topic but also campaigned against those who wanted full transparency. Further investigations by independent journalists exposed both the scandal and cover-up involving the written press, and revealed the unsafe ingredients which were widely in use, as well as bringing to light the wrongful health claims. Things really started to unravel in 1905 when investigative journalist Samuel Hopkins Adams published a ten-article series on the scandal in American magazine *Collier's* entitled *The Great American Fraud*, with the last being printed in February 1906. Pressure on the government to pass a federal law reached an all-time high, and on June 30, 1906, with the backing of President Theodore Roosevelt, the Pure Food & Drug Act came into play, taking action against fraudulent and misleading claims, as well as those who would use unsafe ingredients in their formulations. Almost overnight many companies disappeared, but others, including those that were legitimate and didn't use unsafe ingredients, struggled on despite the fact they were facing further challenges from elsewhere. The dependency on bitters consumption as a medicine was decreasing and a change in taste would signal a shift from strong, bittersweet, spiritous beverages to lighter, citrus-heavy drinks. However, the biggest contributor to their ultimate downfall in the United States was still to come in the shape of the Volstead Act, commonly referred to as Prohibition.

While many parties were ultimately involved in the passing of the Volstead Act, the Women's Christian Temperance Union were the most vocal supporters of a nationwide ban in the US on the manufacture, sale, and transport of intoxicating liquors, citing its effects on women and children. Remaining in place between 1920 and 1933, Prohibition drove the alcohol business underground and into the hands of gangs, most famously those of Al Capone. Any bitters companies that had survived up to this point, such as Boker's, were doing so purely on the strength of their proven medicinal claims or on the finances they'd previously built up. Companies based outside the US and those who weren't solely dependent on income from that country were unaffected, but there were few of these given the huge market in the US for patent medicines.

Figure 1. (opposite) An example of a Victorian medical trade card, complete with questionable health claims

I myself own a bottle of Prohibition-era Egon Braun Hamburg Amargo Bitters, which had traveled through Canada and was stamped and approved by US customs as being acceptable solely for medicinal use. The most notable winner throughout the turmoils of bitters over the centuries was undoubtedly Angostura Bitters due to their location in Venezuela and then Trinidad & Tobago, and also as a result of the success they'd gained with the British Royal Navy and the British Empire more widely. Reflecting on the period, I'm also drawn to the story of Tom Nelsen, then owner of Nelsen's Hall & Bitters Pub in Wisconsin, USA, which is still open to this day. When Prohibition was passed in 1920 Nelsen didn't seek to shut down his bar, instead applying for a pharmacist license so he could serve bitters as a *"stomach tonic for medicinal purposes."* Even in the face of protests to his successful application, as some saw it as a way around the laws to still legally serve alcohol, Nelsen approached the judge at a subsequent court hearing with a measure of bitters and asked him to sample it, questioning if anyone in their right mind would go out of their way to drink it as beverage alcohol. The judge couldn't drink it and Nelsen was released without charges.

In fact, upon learning of Nelsen's story, his nephew Gunnar started a bitters club at Nelsen's Hall, offering shots of Angostura Bitters to patrons. Those who successfully finished the shot became part of their bitters club, receiving a card which read *"This certifies that [insert member's name] has taken "the Cure" by consuming the prescribed medication of bitters and as such is a fully initiated member of the BITTERS CLUB. You are now considered a full-fledged islander and are entitled to mingle, dance, etc. with all the other Islanders."* The card was then stamped by the bartender who dipped his thumb into the empty shot glass and then made an Angostura thumbprint on the card. Tom Nelsen himself drank a pint of bitters per day and lived until he was 90 years old, so there may well be something in the health-giving properties of bitters!

Figure 2. New York policeman dispose of illicit liquor in 1921

THE REBIRTH OF BITTERS

Right up until the turn of the millennium and beyond, if you were to visit most cocktail bars you'd be lucky to find anything other than a dusty bottle of Angostura and Peychaud's, with the odd bar having an Orange Bitters as well, but the modern resurgence has echoed the growth pattern from their original heyday. In the 19th century, early bitters of the spicy, aromatic variety, namely Angostura, Peychaud's, and Boker's, were later joined by more exotic bottlings such as orange, peach, and celery toward the end of the century. This happened again in the first decade of the 21st century, with the early classic formulations joined by a range adopting a more culinary approach.

Fee Brothers of Rochester, New York, has been involved in the drinks industry since 1863 with a portfolio now boasting over 80 products. Bottles of Fee Orange Bitters from around 1930 are in existence, although you can see the current demand for more varied flavors in their expanded range: Mint, Black Walnut, Lemon, Aztec Chocolate, Grapefruit, Celery, Peach, Plum, Rhubarb, Cranberry, Cherry, Old Fashion, West Indian Orange, Molasses, Cardamom, and Whiskey Barrel-Aged Bitters. Fee Brothers divide the industry with their use of glycerin and synthetic flavorings in some of their products, but they do deserve a lot of credit for keeping interest in the bitters category alive through difficult times.

English bartender and New York adoptee Gary Regan, the respected author of the excellent *The Joy of Mixology*, rightly takes a lot of the credit for kick-starting the renaissance with his **Regans' Orange Bitters No. 6**, which were put into production in 2005 after Regan had spent several years perfecting a recipe influenced by one found in Charles H. Baker Jr's book, *The Gentleman's Companion*, printed in 1939. Having a widely available orange bitters on the market was quite something given their wide use in classic cocktails. Regans' Orange Bitters are produced by the Sazerac Company who also look after Peychaud's.

Around the same time, Robert Petrie, a pastry chef at the Dorchester Hotel in London, began manufacturing his **Bob's Bitters** after being approached by bartender Giuliano Morandin. Petrie was asked to recreate a bitters recipe from the past for the relaunch of The Bar at the Dorchester following its refurbishment in 2005. The initial formulations produced for the reopening were Lavender, Cardamon, Ginger, Coriander, Grapefruit, and Vanilla. Petrie was very taken with the resulting products and dabbled further; today Bob's Bitters manufacture a variety of bottlings which primarily focus on one dominant flavor (known as tincture-style bitters), with Peppermint, Orange & Mandarin, Liquorice, Chocolate, and Abbotts—an historical recreation developed together with Jake Burger of London's Porobello Star and the Ginstitute—now part of his stable.

In 2006, German bartenders Stephan Berg and Alexander Hauck founded **The Bitter Truth** after becoming increasingly frustrated at the lack of bitters available in the European market. They now produce a line very much in the classic style of spiced and

Figure 3. (above) A selection of varieties from Bob's Bitters

fruit-based bitters, including Old Time Aromatic, Jerry Thomas' Own Decanter, Original Celery, Orange, Lemon, Hopped Grapefruit, Chocolate, Peach, Tonic, Cucumber, and Creole Bitters.

Then 2007 saw the emergence of **Bittermens** in the US, formed by Janet and Avery Glasser, intertwining traditional bitters practices with a modern approach to flavor combinations, as found in their Xocolatl Mole (*cacao, cinnamon*), Grapefruit (*hops, grapefruit peel*), 'Elemakule Tiki (*cinnamon, allspice, paprika*), Boston Bittahs (*chamomile, citrus, salt*), and Burlesque Bitters (*hibiscus, berries*).

Figures 4 and 5. (above and opposite) Bottlings from The Bitter Truth and Dr. Adam Elmegirab's bitters

2009 saw the emergence of two further bartender-owned brands. In Seattle, Miles Thomas started **Scrappy's Bitters**, which have since gained a worldwide following. The signature, Lavender Bitters, is now accompanied by Grapefruit, Orange, Cardamom, Chocolate, Celery, Lime, Black Lemon, Orleans, and Aromatic Bitters, a portfolio combining classic-style bitters and dominant single flavors.

I'd be remiss if I failed to mention my role, and my own bitters, in this story. Also in early 2009, **Dr. Adam Elmegirab's** came to be, through a successful bid to reformulate Boker's Bitters, which had disappeared during Prohibition. The plan had been to focus on bitters which had an all-round flavor profile (think citrus, floral, vegetal, or earthy), in lieu of centering on a single dominant flavor. The line now runs to include Dandelion & Burdock (*dandelion root, burdock root, citrus peel, ginger, anise*), a reformulated Spanish Bitters (*chamomile, citrus, coriander, orris root*), Aphrodite Bitters (*chocolate, cacao, coffee, ginger, chili*), Teapot Bitters (*black tea, yerba mate, baking spices*), and Orinoco Aromatic (*quassia, chamomile, orange, cardamom, cinnamon, raisins*). As I understand it, my brand was the first in history to openly reveal the contents of each bottling.

I've highlighted and focused on the above brands as, for me, they are the leaders in the global market, with the widest exposure and the most common products I see on my travels, although it should be acknowledged that there are dozens of new brands appearing and disappearing on an almost monthly basis across the world. To cover each brand would require a book in its own right, something attempted by the aptly named Mark Bitterman with his 2015 *Field Guide to Bitters and Amari*, though it already requires an update with the numerous changes since! The bitters category has seen growth akin to that in the gin and beer worlds, with demand and innovation driving each other forward. Certain producers have focused on their home markets and shown no real desire to branch out, while others haven't seen enough growth to sustain a viable business. In the US, for example, it wouldn't be surprising to find that each state has at least one producer.

The bitters category is still relatively small and hasn't really captured the imagination of the global drinks' conglomerates and spirit brands, but they are watching and their interest is growing. The Bitter Truth have collaborated with two Pernod Ricard brands, Havana Club and Beefeater, to produce custom bottlings. In 2017 Bittermens sold a stake to the Sazerac Company in what is being called a "strategic interest," and my own brand has collaborated with Belvedere Vodka, Black Bottle Whisky, and Caorunn Gin to produce bespoke bottlings for them. Further interest from others has also been forthcoming so don't be surprised to see more growth and expansion for bitters producers. Many of the main players are branching out to manufacture other products outside the world of bitters, but which have a synergy with their existing output, namely a variety of botanical-influenced items such as liqueurs, amari, and apéritif- or digestif-styled liquids.

"Making bitters is easy," they said.

At this point in the book many readers will likely be expecting to find a recipe, or recipes, to produce your own bitters at home; I'm going to cover this from a different angle, and I'll explain why.

Many books published prior to this have primarily regurgitated the same style of recipe, guiding you to (i) simply place a variety of botanical matter in high-proof alcohol and macerate it for a period of time, (ii) to use alcohol typically in the 45–50% ABV ballpark, and (iii) to direct you oddly to cook spent botanicals in water, then add this water to infused spirit to dilute to bottling strength. These simple misdirections are flawed, firstly because maceration isn't necessarily the best means of extracting flavor from botanical matter, secondly because, even though the alcohol is high-proof at around 45–50% ABV, the other 50–55% of the contents is water, which does not make for the best solvent. Ultimately you want a higher alcohol strength for a fuller flavor extraction. And lastly, because the process of cooking some botanicals in hot water can extract pectin and leave you with a bitter jelly, not a bitter liquid; additionally the cooking process can ruin some of the subtle nuances you wish to obtain from your selected botanical recipe.

Now don't get me wrong, these recipes can on occasion provide you with a satisfactory result and give you some idea of what's involved in the production of bitters. However, they don't address some of the immediate concerns and focuses one should be looking to tackle. The manufacture of bitters, as with all alcohol production, is a costly exercise with base spirits typically being heavily taxed and quality botanicals such as vanilla, saffron, and orris root being very expensive to purchase. Also, the time involved to produce a quality bottle equal to that which is already available off the shelf is lengthy. Research on whether a botanical is safe to consume, and in what ratio, also needs consideration, which again can offer conflicting results depending on where you look. As an example, tonka bean is banned by the US Food & Drug Administration (FDA) due to the fact that it contains coumarin, which can be harmful if consumed in large amounts, but given tonka's wide usage in the culinary world and the way it is actually consumed, in very, very small doses as a flavoring or garnish, the risk is all but void. For comparison, nutmeg has no such ban and is also poisonous if consumed in large amounts. Thankfully the European Union and the FDA are generally in agreement, providing enough guidance on their websites to keep you on the right track, but as demonstrated with tonka bean you'll find conflicting opinion and will ultimately be left to your own devices. When this happens, the rule I've always stuck by is to try things if it's solely for my own consumption, but if manufacturing products for the consumer, steer clear of anything which has doubt.

My main focus is also going to be on the style of bitters we perceive as "true" or "classic"—that's high-ABV spirit, natural botanicals, water, and sugar if required. It won't involve any preservatives, synthetic flavorings, or colorings. Now, if this still has you interested in making your bitters (the knowledge and skills I'll show you can be transferred to the production of fortified wines, liqueurs, and amari), read on. I'll do my utmost to cover all considerations.

> " MAKING BITTERS IS EASY, " THEY SAID.

WHY MAKE YOUR OWN?

Firstly, ask yourself why you have begun this undertaking because, and trust me on this, it's going to cost you a lot of time and money to get right. There are currently hundreds, if not thousands, of perfectly good bitters flavors on the market so, unless it's something which isn't currently available, is it really worth the expense and time? Bitters' companies have decades' worth of experience, and even the newer ones such as my own, Bittermens, and The Bitter Truth now have 10-plus years' worth of experience, expensive production equipment, and countless records of laboratory analysis to ensure products are world-class, and most importantly safe to consume. A bitters blend of readily available product can more than suffice in providing you with your target flavor profile, say for example if you wanted a chocolate orange bitters, and current producers may even be willing to collaborate with you on a project—logistics and volume pending. Some may interpret this as a bitters' producer putting off potential competition, but that's far from the case—I welcome the category gaining strength. I simply want to provide you with an understanding of the realities of spirit production, and they would be the same questions I'd be asking if I wanted to start making beer, gin, liqueur, or any form of alcoholic product.

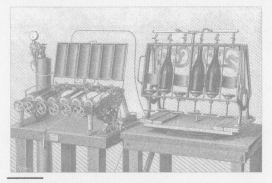

Figure 6. Victorian bottling equipment

IS IT LEGAL?

I can hear you screaming, *"Just give us the damn production info!"* but the legality is something which has to be considered and taken very seriously. I'm no legal expert on every law covering every country in the world, but in most cases you'll have no problem making bitters at home so long as you are making it for yourself, or for sale and consumption within the confines of your own bar, but there are exceptions to that rule. At the time of writing, there are some states in America where it is illegal to infuse or alter the taste of purchased alcohol, and that classification obviously covers home-made bitters. If you're looking to sell off premises, or outside your home, you will unquestionably require some form of licensing wherever you are in the world, whether it be food safety-related or simply for producing and selling alcohol. The production of alcohol equals tax, and governments don't miss a beat when it comes to cold, hard cash. Seek legal advice if necessary, ensure you communicate with local and national authorities to cover your back, and ready yourself for a lot of frustration—many laws and regulations covering production are archaic, although they seem to be changing and progressing with the growth in cocktail culture. Don't say I didn't warn you, though.

IS IT SAFE?

So you've come this far, have a killer idea for a bitters which is going to shake up the world, secured a budget from your bar owner to bring the idea to reality, have a friend ready to design your label, obtained a compounder's licence from HMRC, and registered your business with the local food safety authority (*both UK relevant*). *Woodrow's Tobacco & Cinnamon Bitters* is going to change the Old Fashioned cocktail game in bar rooms across the world, you think!

No.

No, no, no.

Just no.

Nope.

This is an example I see regularly on my travels. A bar making their own bitters using tobacco. Think about that for a second. Tobacco. Infused. Bitters. There's a wealth of information on the Internet covering the dangers, but without even looking we all know that's not going to be safe, and will potentially harm someone or make them very sick. So before you start manufacturing anything, ensure you carry out the correct due diligence to ensure that every ingredient you wish to use is safe. The FDA's GRAS list (*Generally Regarded As Safe*) and EU guidelines will keep you on the right track.

When I started dabbling with bitters production in 2006, very much a novice with only basic knowledge, I wrote down a list of common botanicals used in everyday food and drink—think citrus peels, star anise, cloves, chamomile flowers, coriander seed, caraway—and then added to it using a list of ingredients sourced from a book printed in 1897. This older list of botanicals included the likes of calamus, cassia, cinnamon, cinchona, tonka, tansy, snakeroot, coumarin, and sassafras. I regularly see this latter list of ingredients referenced in modern recipes, and in discussions on social media or Internet forums. However, among this list, snakeroot is highly toxic, tonka is banned in some cases (as mentioned previously), and cinchona is mostly safe but can do serious damage in the wrong hands. I cannot stress the importance of ensuring every ingredient you use is safe for consumption and, again, if you have any doubts or can't clarify it, ignore it and move on.

The most common solvent used in the production of bitters is high-strength ethanol. With its ability to bond with water and fat-soluble molecules, ethanol is extremely effective in extracting and preserving both flavor and aromatic compounds, which is why it's used in the production of alcohols such as gin, as well as in medical drugs and perfume manufacture. As a general rule of thumb, the higher the ABV, the more effective the extraction, though it should be noted that higher strengths of alcohol can pull out flavors and extremely bitter notes which may not be desired from specific botanicals. However, stringent monitoring can nullify this issue. The starting ABV of your base spirit should be kept relatively high (above 60% is preferable) but how high you go will really depend on the botanical matter in your formula, because different strengths of ethanol will have differing results, say in how it interacts with delicate dried flowers versus bold spices such as cloves or anise. I advocate making small tinctures of botanicals—that's a single botanical in the spirit—and testing each separately to see how they interact in varying ratios and in varying ABVs before combining together for your bitters recipe. As I've acknowledged previously, this is a costly exercise but if you want to make the best-tasting product money is no issue.

Should your end goal be to make a bitters which qualifies as non-alcoholic, then you'll need to use glycerin as your solvent in place of ethanol. Glycerin is a type of sugar alcohol and mildly sweet in taste, which can throw off the taste of bitters formulas. I therefore recommend counteracting the sweetness of glycerin with additional bitter botanicals. The most recognized producer that uses glycerin in their formulas are Fee Brothers from Rochester, New York, although it should be noted that ethanol is also used in some of their formulations.

BOTANICALS

You want to use 100% natural botanicals, dried in most cases. Fresh botanicals can be desirable, for instance fresh citrus peel in the production of a citrus bitters, but it all depends on the flavor profile you intend to capture. Dried lemon peel and fresh lemon peel are both incredibly tasty but offer wildly different results.

The botanicals you choose from are commonly herbs, spices, roots, and barks, examples of each being dill, cloves, dandelion root, and cinnamon, although uncommon ingredients such as Earl Grey tea, cacao nibs, coffee, and chili peppers are increasingly making their way into recipes. A typical formula will consist of a bitter botanical alongside a primary flavoring or flavorings, which will form the backbone of your recipe, and in some cases a natural aroma fixative to preserve and retain aromatic qualities, the most well-known examples being angelica, orris root, and anise. The bittering agent will include the likes of quassia bark, gentian, cinchona, rhubarb root, dandelion root, wormwood, or burdock root, all of which possess varying degrees of bitterness and a range of tastes. The dominant flavoring options are endless, but I recommend going for something which has some form of association with bitterness. Watermelon Bitters may sound good in theory, but they don't really make much sense on this front and have limited application.

The supporting cast of botanicals is there to enhance and complement the dominant flavors, some of which can come from the bitter botanical as mentioned, and will be selected solely on how they back up the dominant flavors you're looking to highlight. An example from my own portfolio would be Aphrodite Bitters, created as a tongue-in-cheek stab at the original medicinal history of bitters, and whose ingredients are a nod to supposed aphrodisiacs. The bittering agent is gentian, the primary flavorings are coffee, chocolate, and cacao, all of which are complementary in flavor to each other, and the supporting cast is ginger root, red chilies, allspice berries, and black pepper.

You don't want to use synthetic flavorings or colorings. You just don't.

Figure 7. Nutmeg and mace blades

EXTRACTION

Seemingly unbeknown to those who've provided recipes in the past, there is more than one way to extract flavor from botanicals beyond maceration, which is undoubtedly the most common method in the production of bitters. The method you may wish to use to extract flavor will be entirely related to the equipment you have at hand and how much time you have to dedicate to the process.

MACERATION: In the bitters-making process this is the extraction of essential oils and flavor by soaking botanical matter in a solvent. You take a specific weight of botanical matter, add it to your solvent (most commonly alcohol), and let it rest for a period of time, agitating it regularly to enhance the extraction process. It's not too dissimilar to making a cup of tea using a room-temperature liquid in place of hot water, though the results take substantially longer. Your main variables to consider are the ABV of solvent, the ratio of botanicals to solvent, how fine you wish to grind, crush, or cut your botanicals, and the length of time to macerate your botanical matter in the solvent. Most producers who adopt this method (myself included) advocate a one-pot method, which involves adding all your botanicals at the same time. I argue (and have proven in numerous tastings) that this creates a more complex flavor profile with the various flavors being fully integrated with each other. However, there is a minority who adhere to and believe in making separate tinctures and blending these individual liquids to create their products. Similar approaches to both methods also exist in the production of gins and fortified wines.

PERCOLATION: This is the method of slowly passing a solvent through a filter, in this case a filter packed with ground botanical matter. The most common example we see on an almost daily basis is in the production of espresso coffee where hot water passes through tightly packed coffee grounds, picking up soluble flavors as it moves through. Though much of their production processes are kept secret, it is known that Angostura Bitters are produced using the method of percolation, forcing a heated sugarcane distillate through finely ground botanicals before transferring the liquid to another container where sugar and distilled water are added prior to bottling. Though it is something I've been experimenting with myself, as far as I am aware the percolation method isn't as widely used as you would expect it to be given the reduction in processing time. I imagine this is directly related to the art of bitters production being lost for many years and because producers have largely been secretive about their processes through the decades. As knowledge, and crucially finances, continue to develop and grow within the category don't be surprised to see more brands adopt the percolation method as part of their production processes.

DISTILLATION: This is the process of heating and cooling a substance to separate a solvent (in this case alcohol) from a solution (water), while also extracting and separating crucial essential oils and flavors into the end product. The purity of distilled spirits—think of the clean, crisp flavors found in gin—is one that is desired and celebrated in the beverage industry but not necessarily ideal for the production of bitters for the main reason that the taste of bitterness cannot be distilled. Some people claim it can, and is, but having spoken to a number of distillers and sampled various distilled botanicals, I don't believe it does. Absinthe is a good example of a distilled beverage which contains a substantial volume of a bitter botanical, in this case wormwood, and I've yet to find one which shows any sign of containing bitterness beyond the bitter taste of alcohol and perceived bitter flavors which are there by association. In the world of amari and bitter liqueurs, which are very closely related to bitters, distilled products are commonly used in conjunction with a macerated botanical liquid, with a distillate or range of distillates blended with a bitter maceration to offer the desired bitter taste. An example of this method can be witnessed in the production of the Swiss bitter apéritif called Suze, which takes its dominant flavor from bitter gentian root, combining pressed juice from the root with a complex botanical distillate and a second gentian distillate.

FILTRATION

Just when you thought the end was near, there's one final step you'll have to tackle and this is one that stumps many due to the complications involved. A quick search on the Internet will reveal many who've come unstuck with this last process, because after diluting their bitters to bottling strength their liquid has become cloudy, similar to the louching of absinthe when water is added. I won't get too scientific here, again as the information behind it is fairly lengthy and technical with many variables to consider, but I will offer some perspective and insight as to the best way it can be tackled.

The following example is purely theoretical and relates to very small batches of product:

After macerating around 3.5oz/100g of botanical matter in approximately 34oz/1 liter of 75%-ABV

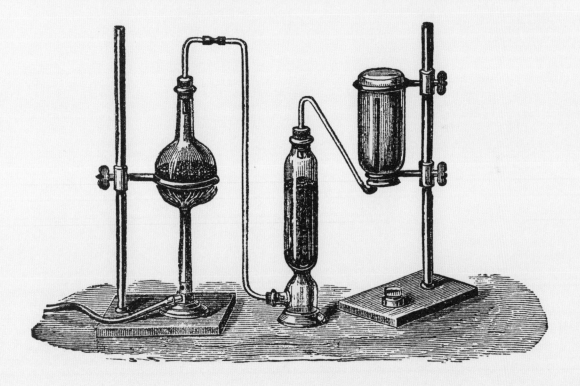

Figure 8. An engraving from "Lessons in Elementary Chemistry" by HE Roscoe, published in 1891

grain neutral spirit, you pass the liquid through a fine strainer/sieve to extract larger pieces of botanical and press them to extract every last drop of your bitters. Following early experiments you wish to reduce the bitters down to 40% ABV, thus calculating you will need to add 30oz/0.875 liters of water. Upon doing so, the bitters, which previously had perfect clarity, are now cloudy. So what's happened here, and what do you do about it?

Simply put, what you've extracted from the botanicals was previously soluble in the higher ABV of spirit at 75%, but this has now dropped out of suspension as the extracted oils and flavors are not soluble in water, with the water content having risen from 25% to 60% now the bitters are 40% ABV. To tackle it, you could either increase the ABV of the bitters to a level where the extracts did not drop out of suspension by adding more of the original macerated product, or you could adopt a fining technique as used in the manufacture of beer and wine. Fining relates to the suspended solids that you're wishing to filter out (i.e. the cloudiness), which will likely have some form of electrical charge, either positive or negative. The introduction of a fining agent, which will also have a positive or negative charge, will bond to an opposing electrical charge like a magnet, become heavy, and then settle at the bottom of your liquid before you filter to remove the solids. Fining agents include bentonite (*negative charge*), egg white powder (*positive*), and gelatine (*positive*). Lactose powder, casein powder, and potato starch powder are also effective, though as you'll most probably be tackling both positive and negative electrical charges, a filtration powder may be preferable, made up of more than one fining agent which offers both positive and negative

YOU STILL THINK MAKING BITTERS IS EASY?

charges. One such powder is described in the *Standard Manual of Soda and Other Beverages* and is made up of 2oz (56g) of egg white powder, 2oz/56g lactose powder, and 1oz/28g of potato starch powder. It recommends adding 1oz/28 g *"of the powder to each gallon of the liquid to be clarified. Let stand in a warm room for a few days, agitating occasionally. Finally, filter through paper."* For the final filtration, which you will setup to filter out the filtration powder, a 10-micron* coffee filter may be suitable, though the solution might require being passed through the filter with captured sediment more than once to extract all the detritus. Sourcing lab-grade filter paper with a lower micron rating, between 1–5, would be an ideal scenario.

Effective filtering will remove all debris, though consideration has to be made for dietary and allergy reasons, especially in this day and age of transparency and heightened regulations. If you are using a fining agent which may go against someone's dietary choice, or could potentially affect someone's health because of an allergy, I advocate full disclosure even if it is not necessarily required as detailed in EU food labeling guidance:

"In the case of wine and wine fining agents derived from egg and milk, EU Regulation No. 579/2012 will need to be considered. In determining whether egg and milk fining agents are still present in wine, they should not be found at the limit of detection (<0.25mg per liter) as indicated in EU Regulation No. 579/2012. Where egg or milk fining agents are not detected at these levels, they are exempt from the allergen labeling requirements."

The filtering process I use in the manufacture of Dr. Adam Elmegirab's Bitters involves the botanicals first being added to a food-grade filter sack (think of it as a teabag of sorts), which is submerged in grain neutral spirit for a period of time, and agitated regularly, until the desired flavor profile is reached. The sack is then removed and the botanicals pressed to extract all the liquid, thus completing the first filtration. The botanicals are passed on to a local farmer for composting, and the bitters diluted to bottling strength with soft Scottish water before it goes through a secondary filtration. This is an air compressor and a self-priming centrifugal pump working in conjunction to pass the bitters through a filter house, first containing a 20-micron filter cartridge to remove larger pieces of particulate, and then secondly through a 5-micron filter cartridge to remove all fine sediment, readying the bitters for bottling. This type of process and equipment will not be uncommon for commercial producers.

You still think making bitters is easy?

* *Furthermore, the aforementioned micron rating is relative to the size of the openings on a filter. Coffee filter papers which are typically between 10 and 20 microns will let larger particulate pass through versus a 5-micron filter, though filters rely on a "nominal" and "absolute" rating, nominal being what could be captured with a success rate between 50–90 percent, while absolute has a success rate of 98.7 percent. If you're ever buying a filter based on its micron rating, you need to ascertain which of these it is, nominal or absolute. For context: the width of a human hair is around 100 microns, while humans cannot see smaller than 40 microns with the naked eye.*

Figure 9. (above) A Victorian chemist at work in a spice factory, circa 1892

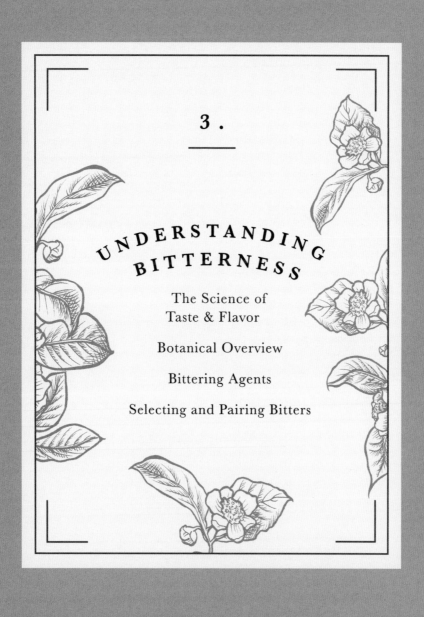

3.

UNDERSTANDING BITTERNESS

The Science of
Taste & Flavor

Botanical Overview

Bittering Agents

Selecting and Pairing Bitters

THE SCIENCE OF TASTE AND FLAVOR

It's widely appreciated that the science behind what we taste and our perception of flavor is extremely complex. It factors in all five of our primary tastes (bitter, salt, sweet, sour, and umami) and our four senses (what we see, hear, smell, and touch), while our personal understanding and appreciation of flavor is based on a whole host of variables, including the likes of previous experience, the environment, temperature, nostalgia, and how we're feeling at the time.

Research into taste and flavor is heavily funded and ongoing, with our wider understanding of both developing on a daily basis and becoming more nuanced as we delve deeper into its many complexities. Notable names, such as French chemist Hervé This and American author Harold McGee have written expertly and endlessly on the subject, so instead of solely presenting scientific study I wanted to approach this subject from a different angle, looking at things from my own personal perspective, which I believe everyone will be able to relate to and draw parallels with. I believe this will help you gain a deeper appreciation of what it is you like and don't like, and the reasons why. It is for this reason that I have selected and grouped the drinks recipes in this book by the five primary tastes, as I am a firm believer that flavor is very personal, continually evolving, and cannot be looked at with a one-size-fits-all ideology.

As I was brought up by a Scottish mother and Middle Eastern father, my appreciation for a wide range of British, Mediterranean, Arabic, and Far Eastern foods developed from a very young age—for example, my tolerance of spicy foods is elevated compared with many of my friends who likely didn't start eating spicier foods until later in life. When cooking a pot of chili for my wife and I, what I deem to taste very mild is abundantly hotter to her, although she is growing to love spicier foods. Our tastes change as we age, and I believe we should continually test our palates, revisit things we weren't sure of previously, and truly enjoy the diversity of tastes and flavors throughout our lives.

▷ ▷ ▷

Figure 1. (opposite)	――― i Apricot blossom ii Gentain iii Pendennis Club Cocktail (see page 124) iv Apricot v Lime vi Cherry

i

ii

iii

iv

v

vi

TASTE

In the dedicated recipe sections that follow, I cover each of the five tastes. Simply put, taste is what happens when our taste buds are stimulated prior to sending signals to the brain to process what we are ingesting. Those tiny bumps on your tongue, collectively known as papillae, are each covered with taste buds containing the receptor cells that send those signals to our brains. Taste buds are found all over your tongue and, contrary to popular belief, each taste can be detected no matter which part of the tongue comes into contact with stimuli, though certain areas do have larger concentrations of taste receptors.

SIGHT

"The first bite is with the eyes" is a phrase often uttered by bartenders and chefs alike, and for good reason. If something isn't visually appealing it will be off-putting, but this goes farther, with everything we see influencing the perceived flavor. The color of a liquid or garnish influences us, but we can be easily tricked; for example, clarified Bloody Marys have long been developed by bartenders, with guests expecting the sensation of a refreshing, ice-cold drink upon being presented with a crystal clear liquid, but instead being hit with the rich mouthfeel of tomato juice and intense spices. The shape of the vessel a drink is served in is also important; there's a reason a large dram of whisky just tastes *better* when enjoyed from a heavy rocks glass; our eyes play a major role in our enjoyment of food and drink and in setting up our expectations.

SMELL

If the first bite is with the eyes, the second is undoubtedly with the nose, with aromatics and our associations with them crucial to establishing whether we will happily consume a specific foodstuff or beverage. The exact figure isn't known but it's said around 80 percent of flavor is unraveled by what we smell, not by what we taste, and for me aroma has always predominantly triggered memories of past experiences, those experiences being decisive in the language we use to describe flavor. Consider lavender: for some it reminds them of summer afternoons playing in fields, running through fresh lavender plants and releasing the pleasant aromatics, but for others, it takes them back to the smell of a grandmother's pot pourri and being stuck indoors with family when they'd rather be playing outside. That genuine sense of puzzlement when I smell something new for the first time, searching deep into the memory bank to figure out what it reminds me of, is a wondrous thing. By the same token, the aroma of food or drink that brings about memories of a negative experience, maybe food poisoning or over-indulging on a specific type of alcohol perhaps, is enough to turn your stomach. Sorry, Southern Comfort, we can't be friends.

SOUND

I've long suspected the loud noise of bars and clubs has an impact on how a drink tastes, and have always maintained that the perceived strength of a beverage is tempered in a noisy bar compared with drinking the same at home, and recent studies have backed up my suspicions. This suppression of taste, coupled with drier cabin air, has been a conundrum for the airline industry for decades with loud background noise being linked to the suppression of sweetness and saltiness, while heightening umami, with bitter and sour flavors largely unaffected. This may be the reason why so many are drawn to tomato juice during flight, something that happened to me on a flight in 2006 when sampling a friend's Bloody Mary, a beverage I'd previously disliked. I've also discovered certain fragrant botanical flavorings such as cardamom are more intense during flight. The coriander seed in Bombay Sapphire gin is more prominent at 39,000 feet—look out for it on your next flight, especially if the airline is serving Indian or Thai food, or if your favorite G&T doesn't taste like it usually does.

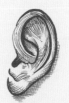

Studies also show that sweetness is enhanced when combined with high-pitched sounds, and that bitterness is heightened when linked with low-pitched sounds, which may explain why whiskey and rock music go together so well.

TOUCH

The importance of touch is no more highlighted than when considering in which vessel to serve a drink. I'll be the first to admit there is something enjoyable about drinking expensive beverages from cheap reusable cups, but the experience is infinitely heightened when imbibing from the appropriate glass. An elegant Champagne coupe, vintage stemmed cocktail glass, or a heavy beer tankard are all great examples of the vessel directly impacting on the drink contained within. The best example from recent memory are the glasses used at London's Bar Termini. Modeled on the type of café bar you'd hope to find on the streets of Italy, they serve the most incredible drinks in these really delicate cocktail glasses which you feel you could easily crush between your fingers. Whether intentional or not, it almost serves to remind you to be more relaxed and take a few minutes to yourself, really enjoy your drink and the surroundings, before heading on your way back on to the bustling streets of London.

To conclude, there are many factors to consider when trying to understand taste and flavor and our relationship with them, but because it's always evolving it's important to accept that it's something we'll never fully get to grips with. Our tasting journey begins from the minute we are born right through to old age, and we should do all we can to make the adventure an enjoyable one, always striving to try something new while celebrating what we truly love.

BOTANICAL OVERVIEW

While the strict definition of botanicals refers to *"A substance obtained from a plant and used typically in medicinal or cosmetic products,"* in the production of alcoholic beverages, and in this case bitters, we are referring to the ingredients utilized in a specific recipe to impart flavor, most commonly herbs, spices, roots, and barks. With the wealth of brands and products available, and with the main focus for most being as a flavoring and not in any way medicinal, the range of botanicals employed currently goes far beyond classic options, with tea, coffee, chocolate, coconut, pineapple, maple, pecan nut, cucumber, and even pumpkin now presenting some formulations.

To cover each botanical that is potentially available for use in bitters would itself require a book-set of encyclopaedic proportions. My predominant aim is to highlight some of the most common ingredients that lend their taste and flavor to your favorite bottlings, so there's a reason some have been excluded, such as calamus and tonka which are known carcinogens. Again I stress the importance of carrying out the appropriate due diligence should you wish to compound your own bitters with a specific fruit, flower, spice, herb, bark, or nut.

Figure 2. (left)
i Quassia plant
ii Apothecary bottle
iii Angelica root

BITTERING AGENTS

———

Primarily roots and barks, but not exclusively, these offer varying degrees of taste and flavor with their main inclusion to impart bitterness, though the flavor of the likes of dandelion root, wild cherry bark, and rhubarb root is also desirable when considering the final flavor profile.

ANGOSTURA BARK
Cusparia febrifuga
Rutaceae

———

Historically used by the natives of South America for its medicinal properties, at the time of writing, over-harvesting of Angostura bark has made it very difficult to obtain, though it should be noted its pungent aroma and flavor aren't necessarily desirable if intended for use on their own. It is no surprise that recipes for Angostura-style bitters from the 19th century, when they were used to treat fever, dysentery, and digestive ailments, were used in tandem with other bitter botanicals and a vast array of flavorsome spices such as cinnamon, cloves, nutmeg, cardamom, and ginger.

CINCHONA BARK
Cinchona succirubra
Rubiaceae

———

Arguably the most consumed bitter botanical in the world today, cinchona bark is widely coveted for its extract—quinine. Quinine is used in the production of bitters, spirits, liqueurs, fortified wines, aromatized wines, and most famously, tonic water, which was likely created as a means of tempering the bitterness of the drug. An effective curative and preventative for malaria, at its height in the 19th century the British Empire was using over 700 tons (635,000 kilos) of the bark every year. Sourcing cinchona and quinine in the UK today is extremely difficult unless prescribed by a doctor, which it often is to deal with leg cramps. Caution is advised when handling cinchona as its 23 species each contains varying levels of quinine. To taste on its own it is very, very bitter and jarring to the palate.

Figure 3. (above) Angostura bark

Figure 4.
Dandelion root

DANDELION ROOT

Taraxacum officinalis

Asteraceae

One of the more delicious smelling and tasting bitter roots, dandelion is bittersweet with a flavor not too dissimilar to mild coffee, with the root often ground down and used to produce a coffee-like beverage. Native to Europe and Asia, it now grows around the globe in the likes of Russia, the US, and Canada. Its most famous usage is in tandem with burdock root in Dandelion & Burdock, originally a fermented drink like beer or mead (honey wine) but now most commonly a type of flavored soda. It is still widely used for its proven medicinal properties.

ANGELICA ROOT

Angelica archangelica

Apiaceae

A historic remedy for digestive problems and used widely in perfumery as an aroma fixative, the stems and dried roots of angelica have long been utilized to flavor bitters and liqueurs, and it is one of the key botanicals found in many gins. The long, thick, twisted roots have an unmistakably earthy aroma, almost musk-like, with a woodsy bittersweet taste.

Figure 5.
Gentian root

GENTIAN ROOT

Gentiana lutea

Gentianaceae

Up there in the debate with cinchona for the most widely used bitter plant in the world, gentian is the key bittering agent in the most famous bitters of them all, Angostura, but is also frequently used in a wide number of bitter liqueurs and amari such as the Italian Campari and the French Suze, Amer Picon, Salers, and Aveze. The English botanist Nicholas Culpeper spoke fondly of gentian, saying *"it comforts the heart and preserves it from fainting and swooning."* Taking its name from King Gentius of Greece, it has been used medicinally for a few thousand years. As the most bitter plant on earth, a little goes a long way, probably explaining why it's used by so many, though the fact it tastes delicious, starting sweet before finishing intensely bitter, helps as well. It's probably my favorite bittering agent.

Figure 6.
Rhubarb root

RHUBARB ROOT
Rheum officinale
Polygonaceae

It is the tart stalks of rhubarb that we're familiar with, thanks to desserts such as Rhubarb Crumble, whereas the oversized leaves are poisonous. It is the root of rhubarb that is called for in bitters production and it has a long history of usage in medicine, mainly as a laxative and digestive aid. The flavor of the root is unique, being both sour and bitter upon tasting. For me the taste and aromatics are not too far away from vinegars and I've always wanted to try the root in the production of Shrubs, a refreshing American colonial drink combining vinegar, fruit, and sugar.

HOPS
Humulus lupulus
Cannabaceae

One of the preeminent ingredients used today in the production of beer, which itself dates back around 9,000 years, the first recorded history of hops being used in the manufacture of beer dates to 822 AD when it started to be used as a flavoring and preservative. Prior to the introduction of hops, brewers used all manner of botanicals to flavor and preserve their beers, with the combination referred to as "*grut*" or "*gruit*." Hop bitters, in the original style of medicinal bitters, could be found in the 18th and 19th centuries, although the first use I'm aware of in the modern cocktail bitters market was in Bittermens' sensational Hopped Grapefruit Bitters. With dozens of hop varieties out there, the potential flavor profiles range from piney to citrus, and from earthy to spicy.

QUASSIA BARK
Quassia amara
Simaroubaceae

Gaining its name from the 18th-century Surinamese botanist Graman Quasi, who used it to treat patients suffering from fevers, quassia bark is still used as an effective antimalarial and in shampoos to combat head lice. Native to the tropical regions of the Americas and the Caribbean, its bitter qualities are utilized today in the manufacture of food and drink; it's the chief bittering agent in Boker's Bitters, both historically and in my modern reformulation. The bitterness imparted by quassia is very sharp and almost astringent, requiring some skill to get the right balance, as too much can really throw a recipe off.

WORMWOOD
Artemisia absinthium
Asteraceae

———

Wormwood has been used in the production of wines and spirits for thousands of years, has been known to take the place of hops in beer, and is a principal flavor in absinthe, which was wrongly blamed for causing many of French society's ills in the late 19th and early 20th centuries, leading to an almost century-long ban based solely on conjecture. Wormwood does contain the toxic compound thujone, but modern scientific research conducted on pre-ban absinthe found that such minute traces make its way into your glass that it's not worth worrying about. Put it this way, by the time you consumed enough to actually cause harm you'd long be dead from alcohol poisoning. Another sharp bittering agent, its menthol-like aromatics and herbal taste lend themselves magnificently to pairings with the likes of fennel, anise, and caraway seeds.

WILD CHERRY BARK
Prunus serotina
Rosaceae

———

Ever wondered why many cough syrups and throat lozenges are cherry-flavored? Well now you know. Though some modern medicines may not explicitly use wild cherry bark in their formulations, many companies such as Vicks still do due to its ability to treat coughs and other ailments, including bronchitis. Also an effective digestive aid, it's been a favorite in the world of herbal medicine for hundreds of years, though its flavor makes it appealing to food and drinks manufacturers as well, with pleasant aromatics and an earthy cherry flavor being dominant.

———

Figure 7.
Wild cherry bark

CITRUS FRUITS

Though typically associated with the taste sensation of sour, the oils and pith found on citrus peels are bitter, while they also contain the flavorings of the fruit, which makes them an ideal choice for bitters producers. Historically, the introduction of citrus and other fruit-based bitters as a dominant flavoring occurred in England in the late 19th century; prior to that they would've been used as a flavoring accent.

BERGAMOT ORANGE

MANDARIN

BITTER ORANGE

MEYER LEMON

BLOOD ORANGE

PERSIAN LIME

CLEMENTINE

PINK GRAPEFRUIT

KAFFIR LIME

SEVILLE ORANGE

KEY LIME

TANGERINE

LEMON

WHITE GRAPEFRUIT

Figure 8.
i Blood orange
ii Pink grapefruit
iii Persian lime

HERBS & FLOWERS

As with citrus fruits, dried herbs and flowers offer both subtle bitterness and complex flavors. These were historically used to accent the dominant flavorings and back up the medicinal purpose behind the bottle, although it's not uncommon nowadays to find products which put these herbs and flowers at the forefront, again with the intended culinary use the priority.

CHAMOMILE FLOWERS

LAVENDER

LEMON VERBENA

PEPPERMINT

ROSEMARY

SPEARMINT

Figure 9.
i Peppermint
ii Chamomile flowers

SPICES

The primary flavorings and most common supporting cast in bitters comes from a variety of spices, with common pairings we see in cooking, such as fennel and anise, cinnamon and clove, or allspice and vanilla, acting as the backbone of many products. Ideas to create your own spice mixes are common, with Middle and Far Eastern cooking reliant on complex blends of spices. Their tried-and-tested recipes, which are often centuries old, should give you the knowledge and inspiration to create a starter point to build from, or to at least understand which spices work to enhance and complement each other.

ALLSPICE BERRIES

ANISE

PEPPERCORNS (BLACK, GREEN, WHITE, RED, AND PINK)

CACAO NIBS

CARAWAY SEEDS

CARDAMOM (BLACK AND GREEN)

CELERY SEED

CEYLON CINNAMON BARK

CLOVES

CORIANDER SEED

FENNEL SEED

GALANGAL

GINGER ROOT

JUNIPER BERRIES

MACE

NUTMEG

RED SANDALWOOD

SAFFRON

STAR ANISE

TAMARIND

VANILLA BEANS (PODS)

Figure 10.
i Juniper berries
ii Pink peppercorns
iii Saffron

SELECTING AND PAIRING BITTERS

—

While there are always exceptions when pairing bitters with specific foods and beverages, there are a few rules and guidelines worth noting that have always served me well when perfecting a recipe or looking to find the right flavor to enhance a drink. Your main objective when selecting and pairing bitters should be to complement and enhance the flavors contained within. Bitters are not intended to be the star of the show—think of them as an orchestra conductor providing direction and keeping everything balanced; and when they're not there, things can go wrong and their presence is missed.

Your attention should first focus on the ingredients a food or drink contains, and the interaction that will take place when combining its primary taste with bitterness, because salt, sweet, sour, and umami each interact with bitterness in a unique way. I've further detailed this in the recipe section, with each drink showcasing the interaction, but the following general rules apply:

BITTER
combined with other bitters will lengthen and accentuate bitterness

—

SWEET
can be used to suppress, or can be suppressed
by the addition of, bitterness

—

SALT
suppresses bitterness

—

SOUR
will be dulled but can temper the taste of bitterness

—

UMAMI
will heighten other flavors while suppressing bitterness

When I started producing bitters in 2009, I was the first bitters brand in history to break with convention and openly discuss the botanical formulation and list the ingredients on the bottle. This stemmed from my background working as a bartender and desiring to know every small detail about the products I worked with. Being largely secretive, bitters companies were never open about what their products contained, which at first made my job purely guesswork, so I wanted to adopt a different approach and to better arm bartenders and consumers with the information they required to make informed choices. As an example, orange bitters work wonderfully well in both dry gin Martinis and sweet rye Manhattans, though in my personal opinion a sweeter orange bitters such as Angostura lends itself better to a gin-based drink, the bittersweet orange notes pairing wonderfully with the common botanicals in gin and the dry vermouth, while a spicier orange bitters such as Regans' No. 6 better suits the coffee, chocolate, vanilla, and pepper in the whiskey, as well as the dried-fruit flavors of sweet vermouth.

If I were to use Tanqueray 10 gin, which contains both chamomile and grapefruit, in a Dry Martini, I may wish to enhance the chamomile and introduce a secondary citrus note, leaving out classic orange bitters and using my own Spanish Bitters, which call for chamomile flowers, lemon peel, and orange peel. This would take the drink down a more floral and citrus route. However, if I wanted to highlight the grapefruit, in which case Bittermens' Hopped Grapefruit Bitters would be perfect. For the Rye Manhattan, the warm baking spices such as cinnamon and allspice are great with orange bitters, but should I want something a bit richer and more indulgent, I might opt for a complementary chocolate bitters, or a coffee bitters, or a chocolate and coffee bitters such as my Aphrodite Bitters. If the objective was to enhance those baking spices, then a classic aromatic bitters such as Angostura, Orinoco, Boker's, Amargo Chuncho, or Abbotts would do the trick. Each of these again works brilliantly with the dried-fruit flavors in the vermouth as well, though you could focus on the dried fruit instead and bring in a cherry bitters, or a plum bitters, or even an apricot bitters. As with all combinations and pairings, it's all about complementing and enhancing. Look at your base spirit and other key ingredients, take note of the key flavorings, or botanicals in the case of gin, and pair those flavors with an appropriate bitters that will result in a drink focused on your desired or favored flavor profile.

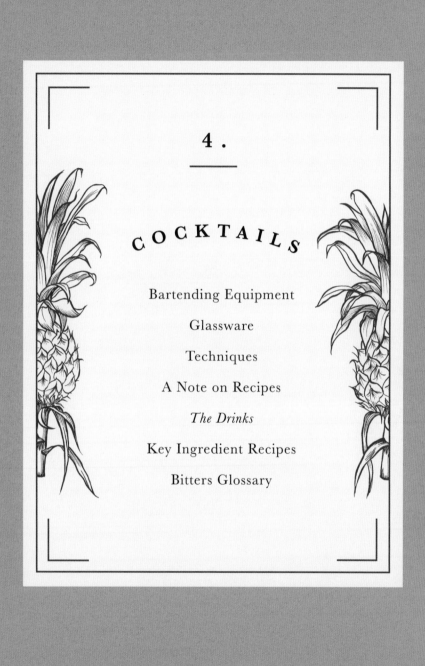

4.

COCKTAILS

Bartending Equipment

Glassware

Techniques

A Note on Recipes

The Drinks

Key Ingredient Recipes

Bitters Glossary

BARTENDING EQUIPMENT

———

With the growing consumer interest in cocktails, coupled with the re-emergence of the career bartender, the wealth and breadth of readily available drink's making equipment sees many furniture and homeware stores stocking cocktail tools alongside those that were previously aimed solely at chefs and home cooks. The ease with which the following pieces of equipment can be obtained is literally at the click of a mouse.

BARSPOONS:
metal spoons which typically have a long spiral handle. A chopstick can be used if you have difficulty handling a barspoon

———

BITTERS BOTTLES:
not a necessity as all bitters brands come with a dasher top and/or pipette but should you want uniformity across the size of dash, you can decant into a separate dasher bottle

———

COCKTAIL SHAKER:
the classic Boston Shaker, the combination of metal and glass halves, is now commonly usurped by metal on metal shakers, two-piece Parisienne shakers, and three-piece Cobbler shakers. The type you use will solely be down to availability and personal preference

———

CHAMPAGNE STOPPER:
you'll need one of these if you don't drink Champagne fast enough!

———

CHANNEL KNIFE:
to be used with fruits and vegetables to make spirals for garnishing

———

CITRUS PRESS:
AKA the Mexican elbow. Available in different sizes, one large enough for lemons and limes and a second large enough for orange and grapefruit will suffice

———

CHOPPING BOARD:
AKA a cutting board, for preparing various garnishes

———

DIGITAL SCALES:
for weighing and measuring ingredients in the preparation of syrups and suchlike

———

FINE STRAINER:
AKA a tea strainer, for removing fine detritus and chips of ice from shaken drinks

———

FUNNEL:
you'll require one to transfer the likes of housemade syrups into clean glass bottles

———

GRATER:
for citrus zest and spices such as cinnamon and nutmeg

HAWTHORN STRAINER:
the most recognizable strainer, used with your cocktail shaker (and fine strainer) to hold
back any large pieces of ice and ingredient debris you have shaken your drink with

---

ICE SCOOP:
so you don't have to use your hands to transfer ice from your freezer or ice well

---

JIGGERS 25 ML / 50 ML OR 1 OZ / 2 OZ:
a double-sided measure

JULEP STRAINER:
used in conjunction with your mixing glass to hold back cubes of ice

---

KNIVES:
for cutting fruit and vegetables, and preparing garnishes

LEWIS BAG:
to be filled with cubed ice and used in conjunction with a wooden mallet to make cracked
and crushed ice. Alternatively, you can wrap ice cubes in a clean kitchen towel

---

MALLET:
to be used in conjunction with a Lewis Bag to make cracked and crushed ice

---

MEASURING JUG:
for measuring larger volumes of liquid, notably in the preparation
of housemade syrups and freshly pressed juices

MEASURING SPOONS:
for measuring smaller volumes of liquid, notably in the preparation of drinks calling for
rich and bold ingredients that require careful handling to ensure balance is maintained

---

MIXING GLASS:
the glass half of a Boston Shaker will suffice, though it is worth investing
in a larger mixing glass to prepare all stirred drinks

MUDDLER:
for pressing fruit, herbs, and spices. A rolling pin will suffice, though the use of muddlers has
decreased in recent years as bartenders opt to use freshly squeezed in lieu of muddled citrus

---

POUR SPOUTS:
not a necessity but useful if you're making large numbers of drinks

---

GLASSWARE

—

The glass is as important as the ingredients in a drink; it contributes to our first impressions and sets up expectations for the drink contained within. Some vessels will also impact on the aromatics, taste, and flavor, depending on shape. The range of glassware available is expansive, so the style you ultimately go for will be purely down to personal aesthetics, but I have offered some suggestions that cover each drink in this book, along with the approximate size required.

CHAMPAGNE FLUTE (240ML / 8OZ):
long-stemmed fluted glass

—

COCKTAIL (150ML / 5OZ):
most commonly associated with the "V"-shaped glass made iconic by the Martini, which I personally hate as it is a nightmare to hold. Visits to antique stores will turn up an incredible selection, though I highly recommend the Nick & Nora style glass for its bulbous shape that's not as shallow as a coupette

—

COUPE (180ML / 6OZ):
commonly used instead of the "V"-shaped Martini glasses in bars nowadays, the Champagne coupe is also the glass of choice for a number of wine sommeliers who champion it in place of the flute

—

GOBLET (300ML / 10OZ):
a footed glass or chalice which can be substituted for a large wine glass

—

HIGHBALL (300ML / 10OZ):
a large, thin glass or tumbler which some often refer to as a Collins glass, probably best known as the vessel most bars will serve a Gin & Tonic

—

PUNCH BOWL (VARIOUS):
a serving bowl which can hold a large block of ice as well as the punch, used in conjunction with a ladle and cups. The required size will solely depend on how many people you wish to serve

—

ROCKS (360ML / 12OZ):
a short tumbler most commonly used for serving spirits such as whisky on the rocks (over ice), these come in various sizes but it is essentially a double rocks you'll require for cocktails served in this type of glass

—

WINE GLASS (360ML / 12OZ):
stemmed glassware that comes in a range of sizes, styles, and shapes

—

TECHNIQUES

———

The preparation of the 50 recommended drinks are all straightforward, being only shaken, stirred, thrown, or swizzled, with any additional groundwork relating to the manufacture of a specific ingredient such as a syrup or in readying a garnish. Every recipe has precise directions in how to produce them detailed, though further information can be found below.

SETTING UP:

———

Ensure all glassware has been cleaned and polished before making any drink. If space allows, all glassware should be chilled in a fridge or freezer before making any drink. Alternatively, you can fill the glass with crushed ice to chill as and when a drink is needed. Cocktails that require a sugar or salt rim, such as A Beer and a Smoke (*see page 109*), should have the rim added prior to chilling, though take into account the method of chilling with crushed ice is not usually desirable with rimmed drinks.

STIRRING:

———

Ensure all required ingredients are at hand. For stirred drinks you will add all the ingredients to your mixing glass before filling it around three-quarters of the way up with cubes of ice. Slide your barspoon in between the ice and glass, then stir for approximately 15–20 seconds or, as a rule of thumb, until the level of liquid and ice are equal. How long is actually required will depend on how dry your ice is at the beginning of the stirring process; for example, if you have taken ice straight out the freezer, you may need to stir for longer or add a splash of water. Before straining into your chilled glass it is worth tasting the drink to ensure it has been diluted and chilled enough; should you feel it needs longer, add some more cubes of ice and stir for a few more seconds. To strain, place a Julep strainer on top of the ice and pour the drink through the strainer's holes into your chilled glassware. Should a drink call for bitters or a rich herbal liqueur such as Green Chartreuse, you may wish to add these first to ensure you have added the correct amount—just so it doesn't throw the balance of a drink if you've accidentally added too much.

SHAKING:

———

Ensure all required ingredients are at hand. As with stirred drinks you will add all ingredients to one half of your shaker, then fill with ice, cap with the other

▷ ▷ ▷

▷ ▷ ▷

half, and shake hard for approximately 10 seconds or until the cocktail shaker is shockingly cold. Again, how long is actually required will depend on how dry your ice is. To strain the drink after shaking, place a Hawthorn strainer over the top of the shaker containing the shaken drink and pour. Should you have added freshly squeezed juices or other solid ingredients such as spices or herbs you will want to pass the drink through a fine strainer when pouring it into your chilled glassware to extract all the detritus. If the drink's ingredients contain fresh egg whites, milk, or cream, you will want to use a technique referred to as dry-shaking—that's first shaking the liquid ingredients without ice for around 5 seconds to fully emulsify the various densities of liquid.

THROWING:

Ensure all required ingredients are at hand. Add all ingredients to one half of your shaker, fill it around three-quarters of the way up with cubed ice, then rest a Julep strainer on top of the ice. Holding the shaker at around head-height, pour the liquid through the ice into the second empty shaker while pulling the empty shaker away from it to aerate the drink. Pour the drink back into the shaker that contains ice and repeat the process five or six times. To finish, pour into your pre-chilled glassware or over fresh ice. This technique is best adopted for wine-based or aromatic ingredients, as well as drinks calling for tomato juice such as the Bloody Mary *(see page 133)*, and works perfectly with two metal shakers due to the thinner rim allowing for a tighter pour.

SWIZZLING:

Ensure all required ingredients are at hand. Add all ingredients directly to your serving vessel, fill with crushed ice, then insert a barspoon or swizzle stick down into the drink to the center of the glass. Clasp your hands together with the spoon or swizzle stick held in between them, and rub together while occasionally moving the spoon or swizzle stick up and down to incorporate the liquid ingredients with the ice, diluting and chilling the drink, but also creating a frost on the outside of the glass. As the drink dilutes you will likely be required to add more ice, especially at the point of service. This technique works best with drinks that have a higher ABV, as the freezing point of alcohol is lower, ensuring you get the desired frost on the outside of the drinking vessel.

A NOTE ON RECIPES

———

I have written this book to enlighten, demystify, and most importantly entertain the reader about the world of bitters. In the pages that follow, I have compiled a selection of cocktails which I believe best demonstrate the role that specific flavors of bitters play in drinks.

With bitterness being only one of five tastes that form the building blocks of mixed drinks, I have grouped these cocktails by those five taste sensations. Bitter first and foremost, then Sweet, Sour, Salt, and Umami. These sensations are individually represented by ingredients crucial to the overall flavor profile of the drink.

All the recipes that follow are a combination of serves which have been around for generations. They have featured on drinks menus around the globe, from Paris to Lima, Chicago to Taipei, and everywhere else in between. They have been consumed hundreds, thousands, and in some cases millions of times, were formulated by some of the best bartenders in the world, have won countless cocktail competitions, and have been tried and tested in a variety of cities on my travels. These recipes are bulletproof and I'd be confident to put them on the menu of any cocktail bar in the world. However, it shouldn't be overlooked that taste is subjective and recipes are no more than guidelines intended to give you a framework to build drinks to suit your own tastes. Whether Sour is your preference, or Sweet, or maybe you prefer it a touch stronger, or stirred longer to be slightly weaker, the ultimate goal is to find the perfect drink and ratio suited to your palate, so please try the recipes as provided, then adjust to your desired taste preference. Sláinte!

BITTER

———

When bitter flavors come into contact with the human tongue this stimulates a sequence of events that culminates in the flow of digestive juices to the stomach, liver, duodenum, and pancreas. This is the reason why they're so heralded for their use in apéritifs, which set you up for a meal, and in digestifs, to aid digestion.

Due to the many layers of flavor they contain, bitters assist in the integration of flavors within cocktails, bridging gaps between the various components, enhancing or complementing existing flavors, and adding layers of complexity, depth, and character. Bitters will temper sweetness and, as detailed in William Boothby's 1908 book *The World's Drinks and How to Mix Them*, will *"remove the sharp, raw taste peculiar to all plain liquors."* Ultimately, as bitter is the most sensitive of tastes, the amount used in a drink will vary from person to person—from those who find bitterness disagreeable to those who actively desire it. Nonetheless, I do believe bitterness can be appreciated and enjoyed over time, and this will largely depend on how it's delivered, from bittersweet/dark chocolate or a shot of espresso to a hoppy IPA.

CORN AND OIL

Paul Lambert, The Blind Pig, Dublin, Ireland

2 OZ / 60 ML GOSLING'S BLACK SEAL RUM

¾ OZ / 22 ½ ML FALERNUM

3 DASHES AROMATIC BITTERS
(*ANGOSTURA, THE BITTER TRUTH
OLD TIME, OR DR. ADAM ELMEGIRAB'S
ORINOCO AROMATIC BITTERS*)

¼ OZ / 7 ½ ML FRESH LIME JUICE

Pour all the ingredients over crushed ice in a rocks glass and swizzle (see page 56). Top with more crushed ice if necessary, then garnish with a wedge of lime and a hint of freshly grated nutmeg (optional).

The origins of this drink are unknown, to the point there is little conjecture to stir debate between cocktail aficionados. The modifier used in this drink, Falernum, also has a mysterious history, but all roads point to it originally being *"a beverage compounded of rum, lime juice, and syrup,"* as detailed in *Transatlantic Sketches in the West Indies, South America, Canada, and the United States* (1869) by Greville John Chester. I believe the addition of spices and botanicals—such as cloves, allspice, star anise, and ginger—to Falernum was a later addition popularized by the John D. Taylor company, thus making it a bottled punch of sorts.

On my travels I regularly discover cities where the Corn & Oil has gained a cult following, Tel Aviv being a notable example. One person who has done as much as anyone to popularize this drink is Paul Lambert from The Blind Pig in Dublin, where his guests, including Malcolm Gosling of Gosling's rum who had traveled from Bermuda, can't get enough of this complex sipper. Imagine turning the flavor of a Rum & Cola up to 11, and it gives you an idea of what to expect: punchy, subtly sweet, warm baking spices, a touch of bitterness, and the perfect level of citrus to round off the edges.

BRANDY CRUSTA

Joseph Santina, City Exchange Bar, New Orleans, USA

2 oz / 60 ML PIERRE FERRAND
    1840 COGNAC (OR VSOP
    COGNAC)

3 DASHES DR. ADAM
    ELMEGIRAB'S BOKER'S
    BITTERS

⅓ oz / 10 ML PIERRE FERRAND
    ORANGE CURAÇAO (OR
    GRAND MARNIER)

⅓ oz / 10 ML FRESH LEMON JUICE

⅓ oz / 10 ML SUGAR SYRUP
    (SEE PAGE 150)

Using a potato peeler, remove the zest from a lemon by starting at one end and winding down in a long spiral. Put the zest to one side, cut the peeled lemon in half, then rub one half round the rim of a small wine glass to moisten, before rolling the rim of the glass in sugar to form the crust. Place the glass in the fridge or freezer to chill. Add all the ingredients to a cocktail shaker, fill it with cubed ice, and shake hard for around 10 seconds. Strain into the pre-prepared cocktail glass and garnish by wrapping the lemon spiral around the inside of the glass.

We humans can't leave a good thing alone, can we? In 1980, John Landis brought us *The Blues Brothers*, a musical comedy starring John Belushi and Dan Aykroyd, which is unquestionably one of the greatest movies of all time. In 1998 they then proceeded to make *Blues Brothers 2000*. The less said about that the better. However, sometimes we do get it right—*The Godfather Part II* anyone? For me, the Crusta is in *Godfather Part II* territory. Don't get me wrong, the Old Fashioned Cocktail is a wonderful drink, but the Crusta takes things to the next level. In my opinion, it is the most overlooked family of drinks around, probably because of the preparation involved in making it. It's worth the effort though. Trust me.

The basic DNA of a cocktail—that's spirit, sugar, water, and bitters if you've forgotten—was taken apart in the 1850s by New Orleans bartender Joseph Santina, who started all over. Replacing water with ice to dilute the drink is standard practice nowadays, but at the time it would've been revolutionary—boxes of insulated ice had only just become available and only to those who could afford it. The addition of flavor accents (*see pages 48–49*) by way of a touch of lemon juice (just enough so that it doesn't encroach into the sour family of cocktails) and orange Curaçao, to add depth alongside the dried fruit, spice, and vanilla typically associated with the brandy or Cognac, added further depth, and the garnish was unlike anything seen before. As we know, the first taste is with the eyes, and few drinks showcase this better, with the lemon peel and sugar crust perfectly setting you up for the drink contained within.

MARTINEZ/MANHATTAN

Unknown origin

2 OZ/60 ML COCCHI VERMOUTH
DI TORINO

1 OZ/30 ML OLD TOM GIN OR
RYE WHISKEY

3 DASHES AROMATIC BITTERS
(ANGOSTURA, THE BITTER
TRUTH OLD TIME, OR DR.
ADAM ELMEGIRAB'S ORINOCO
AROMATIC BITTERS)

1 DASH LUXARDO MARASCHINO
LIQUEUR OR PIERRE
FERRAND ORANGE CURAÇAO

Add all the ingredients to a mixing vessel, fill it with cubed ice, and briskly stir for around 15–20 seconds. Strain into a pre-chilled cocktail glass and garnish with a cocktail cherry or a coin of citrus zest (lemon or orange).

The union of spirit, vermouth, and bitters has long been celebrated in the world of mixed drinks, going back to the late 19th century when the forefathers of these two variants, the Manhattan (gin-based) and the Martinez (whiskey-based), first surfaced in bar rooms in the US and across Europe. The premise is relatively simple: take a spirit, balance it with a ratio of vermouth—sweet, dry, or the less-favored combination of the two (*oddly referred to as perfect*)—and then finish it with bitters, which will enhance and complement the base liquids. In the past, bartenders would add further accents with dashes of syrups and liqueurs such as absinthe, Curaçao, maraschino, and amari. This is practiced less, though, nowadays—something of a surprise because it offers up a more intriguing and complex drink.

Nowadays, we often serve a Martinez or Manhattan with a ratio of two parts spirit to one part vermouth, which does offer up a more intense cocktail. However, I'm a big fan of the older-style serves which tended to offer equal ratios or, as I prefer my Martinez and Manhattan, with two parts of vermouth to one of spirit. The reason behind it is two-fold: firstly, it provides a more flavorful beverage with the myriad of flavors provided by the vermouth, accented and highlighted by the liqueur and bitters of course; and secondly, because it in turn becomes a lower ABV, and therefore a more "sessionable" drink. While I would encourage you to try the vermouth-heavy option, my main advice would be to use an Old Tom gin or whiskey with an ABV of around 45% so that it doesn't get lost in the drink.

KEEP IT IN THE FAMILY

Unlike other recognized drinks families, including the likes of sours, punches, toddies, and flips, to my mind there's never been a recognized name for the assemblage of cocktails made up of the combination of spirit, vermouth, and bitters. This is somewhat odd when you consider the reputation and popularity drinks of this ilk have garnered, although it would explain why the Manhattan and Martini have become catch-all terms. The Vermouth Cocktail seems like a fitting title as the DNA of the Cocktail itself—spirit, sugar, water, and bitters—is virtually intact, although the sugar is replaced with vermouth. Other notable beverages in the Vermouth Cocktail family include the Rob Roy, which has a base of Scotch whisky; the Kangaroo with a base of vodka; the Palmetto with rum; the Turf with genever; the Harvard with brandy; and, of course, the king of them all, dry gin in the Dry Martini (*see page 77*).

KENNEDY MANHATTAN

Carl Wrangel, The Barking Dog,
Copenhagen, Denmark

2 OZ / 60 ML EL DORADO 15-YEAR-OLD RUM

¾ OZ / 22 ½ ML DOLIN BLANC VERMOUTH DE CHAMBÉRY

4 DASHES DR. ADAM ELMEGIRAB'S BOKER'S BITTERS

1 TEASPOON / 5 ML MAPLE SYRUP

Add all the ingredients to a mixing vessel, fill it with some cubed ice, and briskly stir for around 15–20 seconds. Strain into a pre-chilled cocktail glass and garnish with a cocktail cherry.

The Kennedy Manhattan is a modern iteration of the Manhattan created by Carl Wrangel when he previously tended bar in Copenhagen's Oak Room back in 2011. Unpacking a spirits delivery one afternoon, Carl was to find that his supplier had sent the wrong rum, El Dorado 15-year-old instead of their 12-year-old, and the wrong vermouth, Dolin Blanc Vermouth de Chambéry instead of Dolin Dry, so he set about trying to make a cocktail which would best utilize them both. He let the rum take center stage with its flavors of dried fruit, warm baking spices, honey, and gingerbread, which harmoniously complemented the Dolin Blanc, a medium-dry vermouth based on Ugni Blanc wine, with its white-wine acidity and citrus, floral, and fresh, white fruit flavors. Including a teaspoon of maple syrup added further depth and complexity, while the Boker's Bitters, with its intense bitterness and pronounced smoked tea, coffee, cardamom, and orange aromatics and flavor, rounded off the edges and added to the length of the finish.

It takes its name from Carl's friend Sean Kennedy, who was sat at the bar when Carl first made the drink, although he would also later learn that former US President John F. Kennedy was a fan of rum. A tenuous link indeed, but I'm sure this is a drink he would have approved of.

OLD FASHIONED

Unknown origin

2 OZ / 60 ML BUFFALO TRACE
BOURBON

3 DASHES AROMATIC BITTERS
(*ANGOSTURA, THE BITTER
TRUTH OLD TIME, OR DR.
ADAM ELMEGIRAB'S ORINOCO
AROMATIC BITTERS*)

⅓ OZ / 10 ML DEMERARA SUGAR
SYRUP *(SEE PAGE 150)*

*Add all the ingredients to a mixing vessel, fill
it with cubed ice, and briskly stir for around
15–20 seconds. Strain into an ice-filled rocks
glass and garnish with a coin of fresh orange
zest snapped over and dropped into the drink.*

It speaks volumes for the impact and growth of cocktail culture over the last two decades that the Old Fashioned is now a favorite the world over. It has reached the point where bars are no longer required to list it on their menus as their guests are more than aware of its existence, much like the Mojito, Dry Martini, and Cosmopolitan. Put it this way, when I first started bartending in the early 2000s I would've been lucky to make a handful in a year; in the latter years behind the bar in 2012 there were times I was making a handful every few rounds.

Quite simply, the Old Fashioned is an interpretation of and reference to the oldest cocktail ever created, in fact it was the first (*see page 15*). The Old Fashioned harks back to a period in the first Golden Age of mixed drinks—between the 1860s and Prohibition in the US—where patrons simply requested a cocktail made in the old-fashioned way. It is as simple as they come, but it has an intrigue and ceremony around its preparation that makes it an experience unlike almost any other mixed drink. I believe part of the allure is its immersion in popular culture, in recent times most prominently via Don Draper in the American television series *Mad Men*.

You can, of course, use any spirit you wish in an Old Fashioned, but for now we'll focus solely on the Whiskey Cocktail or Whiskey Old Fashioned.

A GENUINE OLD FASHIONED?

Now, I wish to cover the two different debates that continue to surround the preparation of the Old Fashioned. The first is whether you should use a combination of a rough-cut sugar cube muddled with the bitters and a splash of water (as per George Kappeler's 1895 book *Modern American Drinks*) in lieu of using a pre-made syrup (first featured in Jerry Thomas's *How To Mix Drinks* in 1862). As for including the sugar cube, your main concerns will be related to time and consistency. Using a muddled cube can provide a slightly different texture and mouthfeel to the drink which some desire. Either way you will ultimately end with a more palatable measure of whiskey, with the sugar softening the bite of the spirit and the bitters rounding the edges, while accentuating specific flavors found within the whiskey and removing that raw taste found when consuming straight spirits. The second dispute is whether or not to add muddled cherries and fresh orange slices to the simple combo of whiskey, sugar, water, and bitters. Let's shut that down straightaway. If that's the way you wish to drink yours, then all power to you, but it's not a true Old Fashioned, which should simply be spirit, sugar, water and bitters.

TRINIDAD ESPECIAL

*Valentino Bolognese, Pura Vida,
  Bologna, Italy*

1 OZ / 30 ML ANGOSTURA BITTERS

1 OZ / 30 ML ORGEAT SYRUP

¾ OZ / 22 ½ ML FRESH LIME JUICE

⅓ OZ / 10 ML MACCHU PISCO

*Add all the ingredients to a cocktail shaker, fill
it with cubed ice, and shake hard for around
10 seconds. Strain into a pre-chilled cocktail
glass. Garnish with a spiral of lime zest.*

Nope. You didn't read that wrong. The base spirit
for the Trinidad Especial is bitters, but it works.
It really does, so much so that it was the winning
drink from the European heat of the Angostura
Global Cocktail Challenge, held at Mood Bar in
Paris in 2008.

Though a rarity, larger measures of bitters have
long been used in mixed drinks. Jerry Thomas's
Japanese Cocktail from his 1862 bartender's guide

How To Mix Drinks detailed half a teaspoonful
of Boker's Bitters in the recipe. Leo Engel's
1878 book *American & Other Drinks* features three
such examples with his Swizzle calling for one
and a half liqueur glasses of Boker's Bitters; his
Sherry Blush a teaspoonful of Boker's; and his
Alabazam a teaspoonful of Angostura Bitters.
Later, in 1908, The Angostura Fizz appeared in
a booklet produced by Angostura Bitters, with
it again appearing in Charles H. Baker's 1946
Gentleman's Companion alongside the alias The
Trinidad Fizz, the recipe utilizing a full ounce
of the bitters.

During the decades that followed, with cocktail
culture and the use of bitters falling by the
wayside as covered earlier in this book, these
types of drinks all but disappeared, but in recent
years they've come to the fore again. Firstly
came veteran bartender Valentino Bolognese's
Trinidad Especial, and not long after, Giuseppe
Gonzalez from New York's Suffolk Arms with
his Trinidad Sour that replaces the freshness of
pisco with American whiskey. Should you wish
for a drier drink and more spice, then it'll be
rye whiskey you're after, but should you desire
a little sweetness to balance against the bitters,
then bourbon whiskey is what you'll need. Both
variants make for incredibly tasty, but complex,
drinks, although the Trinidad Sour has
undoubtedly received wider attention. I've seen
it on menus everywhere, from my hometown
of Aberdeen to Tel Aviv, and I'd imagine this
is due to Giuseppe's standing in the New York
bar scene which, along with London, influences
much of what happens in bars around the globe.

FLINTLOCK

*Tony Conigliaro, Zetter Townhouse,
London, UK*

FERNET BRANCA, TO RINSE

2 OZ / 60 ML BEEFEATER 24 GIN

5 DASHES DR. ADAM
    ELMEGIRAB'S DANDELION
    & BURDOCK BITTERS

½ OZ / 15 ML GUNPOWDER TEA
    SYRUP *(SEE PAGE 152)*

Add a large cube of ice to a rocks glass and a splash of Fernet Branca to chill and rinse. Add the gin, bitters, and syrup to a cocktail shaker, fill it with cubed ice, and shake hard for 10 seconds. Discard the ice and Fernet from the glass, then fine strain the drink into your drinking vessel. Garnish with a piece of magician's wool.

As detailed on *pages 12–13* the cocktail of spirit, sugar, water, and bitters was preceded in 17th- and 18th-century England by simple drinks such as gin and bitters. This drink harks back to those days with its gin and bitters base, and with its name—taken from the flintlock firing mechanism found in muskets, pistols, and rifles from this era.

From the genius mind of London bar operator Tony Conigliaro, the man behind Bar Termini in Soho, 69 Colebrooke Row in Islington, and Untitled in Dalston, the garnish of the cocktail, by way of magician's wool, is what represents the flash-bang effect of the flintlock mechanism. This drink has a DNA similar to that of the Sazerac *(see page 78)*, but the Flintlock introduces another layer of flavor with the Gunpowder Tea Syrup (which gets its name due to the tea's resemblance to gunpowder pellets), creating an end product which is a lot brighter and packed full of flavors you'd associate with England. The tea-based gin provides a solid foundation with the menthol aromatics of the Fernet, and the savory, vegetal, and spiced notes of the Dandelion & Burdock.

BIJOU

Harry Johnson, New York City, USA

1 oz / 30 ml TANQUERAY GIN

1 oz / 30 ml COCCHI VERMOUTH DI TORINO

½ oz / 15 ml GREEN CHARTREUSE

1 DASH ABSINTHE

1 DASH ORANGE BITTERS

1 DASH AROMATIC BITTERS *(ANGOSTURA, THE BITTER TRUTH OLD TIME, OR DR. ADAM ELMEGIRAB'S ORINOCO AROMATIC BITTERS)*

Add all the ingredients to a mixing vessel, fill it with cubed ice, and briskly stir for around 15–20 seconds. Strain into a pre-chilled cocktail glass and garnish with a coin of lemon zest (snapped over the drink and discarded) and a cocktail cherry.

Although it has gained a loyal following in recent years, the Bijou is very much a drink of the late 1880s. At this time, bars increasingly sought to create a point of difference compared to their rivals, and to cater for increasingly cosmopolitan guests. So, American bartenders turned to Europe and the swathe of spirits, amari, vermouth, liqueurs, and bitters that were available to strengthen their armory, and they added new subtleties and complexities to already established drinks.

Strip it down to its bare bones and the Bijou is simply a riff on the original Martini or Martinez, with a few flavor accents and a healthy slug of Green Chartreuse added. I believe the original specification from Harry Johnson, which called for equal parts of gin, vermouth, and Chartreuse, is too heady and cloying, so I've adjusted the ratio but not so much as to mask the bold Chartreuse. I also recommend serving this cocktail in smaller measures, firstly to ensure the *jewel* is sparkling from the first sip to the last, and secondly in homage to its literal translation from French: *"a small, dainty, usually ornamental piece of delicate workmanship."* Best enjoyed after a large meal, the Bijou is a wonderfully complex, bittersweet cocktail that I'm sure you'll love as much as I do.

PORTER SANGAREE

Jack McGarry, Dead Rabbit Grocery & Grog, New York, USA

6 OZ / 180 ML AMERICAN-STYLE PORTER

3 DASHES AROMATIC BITTERS *(ANGOSTURA, THE BITTER TRUTH OLD TIME, OR DR. ADAM ELMEGIRAB'S ORINOCO AROMATIC BITTERS)*

3 DASHES MACE TINCTURE *(SEE PAGE 153)*

¾ OZ / 22 ½ ML LEMON SHERBET *(SEE PAGE 153)*

Add all the ingredients to a mixing vessel, fill it with cubed ice, and briskly stir for around 15–20 seconds. Strain into a pre-chilled cocktail glass and garnish with a coin of lemon zest (snapped over the drink and discarded) and a light dusting of freshly grated nutmeg.

Many of you will likely be more familiar with the red wine, citrus, and sugar-based *Sangría* which, and you'll see where I'm going with this later, literally translates to "bloodletting," a largely abandoned medical practice involving the removal of blood that was thought to cure illness and disease.

Popularized globally in the 20th century, Sangría's bloodline actually dates back to the early part of the 1700s and the *Sangaree*. Deriving its name from the Spanish word for "blood," *Sangre*, in reference to the color of the drink, Sangaree was originally a combination of fortified wine *(Madeira, sherry, or port)*, sugar, and spices, and was popular with Spanish and English colonies in the Caribbean. By the mid-1800s, notably in Jerry Thomas's 1862 book *How To Mix Drinks*, the Sangaree had become a family of sorts with variants based on brandy, gin, ale, and porter alongside the expected sugar and spice.

Beer cocktails are often met with derision, but the growing craft beer and cocktail scenes have opened up a wealth of opportunity to reclaim the hearts and minds of drinkers as in days gone by. For this serve you'll want to use an American-style porter such as that from Anchor, Sierra Nevada, or Founder's. Offering a base of coffee-, toffee-, chocolate-, and molasses-rich flavors, the beer is somewhat tempered but complemented with the introduction of tangy Lemon Sherbet. Additional depth is added by the intense, warming mace and aromatic bitters, creating a perfect warm-weather serve.

OL' DIRTY BASTARD

Bar Shira, Imperial Craft Cocktail Bar,
Tel Aviv, Israel

1 OZ / 30 ML AMARO MONTENEGRO

1 OZ / 30 ML NOILLY PRAT AMBRÉ
VERMOUTH

½ OZ / 15 ML CYNAR

½ TEASPOON / 2 ½ ML PALO
CORTADO SHERRY

3 DASHES ANGOSTURA
BITTERS

3 DASHES DR. ADAM
ELMEGIRAB'S DANDELION
& BURDOCK BITTERS

Add all the ingredients to a mixing vessel, fill
it with cubed ice, and briskly stir for around
15–20 seconds. Strain into a pre-chilled
cocktail glass.

My work in the world of alcoholic beverages has taken me to many of the established cocktail capitals, such as New Orleans, Paris, and London. Although I always look forward to returning, it can't be understated how much I enjoy visiting somewhere off the beaten track and discovering an established or growing cocktail culture, which is what happened during my first visit to Tel Aviv in 2013. Nestled on the ground floor of the Imperial Hotel and just a stone's throw from the Mediterranean sea, you'll find the Imperial Craft Cocktail Bar, a true corner of escapism that instantly transports you to the type of bar you can imagine existed in a European colony, which is from where this bar takes much of its influence.

Speaking of European influence, you'll be hard pushed to find an apéritif- or digestif-style drink which doesn't contain some form of fortified wine, herbal liqueur, amari, or bitters, and this drink is the perfect marriage of all of these, with its combination of Italian, French, and Spanish ingredients. For an Italian bitter liqueur, Amaro Montenegro leans toward the side of sweet with dominant notes of orange zest, cinnamon, ginger, and vanilla, and these are perfectly complemented with the dried fruit and spice of the rich Ambré vermouth. Additional depth comes by way of the vegetal, herbal, and lightly spiced Cynar. The hint of Palo Cortado adds a nutty, dry finish, which is lengthened with the spicy bitters that also temper the sweet edge to the drink, leaving you with the perfect digestif. As they say while raising a toast in Tel Aviv: *"L'chaim!"*

DRY MARTINI

Unknown origin

2 OZ / 60 ML BEEFEATER GIN

½ OZ / 15 ML NOILLY PRAT DRY VERMOUTH

3 DASHES REGANS' ORANGE BITTERS NO. 6

Add all the ingredients to a mixing vessel, fill it with cubed ice, and briskly stir for around 15–20 seconds. Strain into a pre-chilled cocktail glass and garnish with a coin of lemon zest snapped over the drink and discarded.

Hands-down the most iconic cocktail in the world. So much has been already been written about the Dry Martini that I won't spend too long on its history. However, when you consider that early Martinez recipes (*see page 62*) called for two parts of sweet vermouth to one of Old Tom gin, and the first written Martini recipe from 1888 asked for equal parts of those, it's easy to conclude they're related in some way. The Martini was given its name by the brand of vermouth that widely marketed the drink. The Dry variant would first appear around a decade later and grew in popularity along with a shift in taste preferences toward drier drinks.

For a long time, the Dry Martini largely omitted bitters and contained scant levels of vermouth, offering nothing more than an ice-cold glass of gin. This may be to the tastes of some but it really does offer up an inferior cocktail when compared to one with a generous measure of vermouth and a few dashes of bitters. Thankfully, the reemergence of high-quality vermouths and bitters has seen a growing trend for the true classical style. The trick to finding the ideal Dry Martini for your own tastes? It's simple really: search out the primary botanicals in your favorite gin and pair their flavors with the bitters. For example, Leopold's Gin has a heavy lemon profile which works brilliantly with The Bitter Truth Peach Bitters; with Gin Mare, its pronounced basil and herbal notes make it an ideal partner for Bob's Grapefruit Bitters; and Caorunn gin with its crisp apple, citrus, and floral notes pairs wonderfully with Dandelion & Burdock Bitters. Disregard any notion of shaking the drink, stirring is the way forward, and finish the drink with fresh citrus zest. Perfection.

SAZERAC

Unknown origin

2 OZ / 60 ML PIERRE FERRAND
1840 COGNAC (OR VSOP
COGNAC)

4 DASHES PEYCHAUD'S
BITTERS

⅓ OZ / 10 ML SUGAR SYRUP
(SEE PAGE 150)

3 DASHES ABSINTHE

Add the first three ingredients to your mixing vessel, fill it with cubed ice, and briskly stir for around 25–30 seconds. Add the absinthe to a pre-chilled rocks glass to coat the inside, then strain the drink into it. Garnish with a coin of lemon zest snapped over the drink and then discarded.

Despite the fact that the cocktail had been around for at least 32 years previously, the Sazerac company—producers of excellent rye whiskey and of Peychaud's Bitters, which is commonly found in this drink—maintain that the Sazerac was the world's first cocktail, dating from 1838. Their story goes that New Orleans apothecary Antonie Amedie Peychaud would treat friends to his brandy toddy recipe, which contained the medicinal Peychaud's Bitters. These toddies were made using a measuring cup called a *coquetier*, from which the word "cocktail" is also alleged to have derived. To quote Mark Twain: *"Never let the truth get in the way of a good story."*

There's no doubt that brandy cocktails, in this instance an improved cocktail with the addition of absinthe, were being consumed by the French residents of New Orleans, but there's literally nothing to suggest one of them was called a Sazerac. Tellingly, the first mentions of the Sazerac cocktail in print would not appear until the late 1800s and early 1900s, most notably in William Boothby's 1908 publication *The World's Drinks and How to Mix Them*. This recipe was given to him by Thomas Handy, one-time owner of the Sazerac House in New Orleans, and it listed Sazerac brandy and the obsolete Selner Bitters among its ingredients. Today most bartenders will prepare this drink with the spicier rye whiskey, or by echoing the *DeGroff method*, which combines equal parts of whiskey and Cognac. Both styles offer an equally delicious serve, which goes toe-to-toe with the original Cognac variant. In nearly all cases the absinthe will make or break the drink, offering aromatic accents and a herbal complexity that go some way to confirm its "improved" cocktail status.

QUEEN'S PARK SPECIAL

Unknown, Queen's Park Hotel,
Port of Spain, Trinidad

2 OZ / 60 ML ANGOSTURA 1919 RUM

1 OZ / 30 ML FALERNUM

4 DASHES AROMATIC BITTERS
(ANGOSTURA, THE BITTER
TRUTH OLD TIME, OR DR.
ADAM ELMEGIRAB'S ORINOCO
AROMATIC BITTERS)

1 OZ / 30 ML FRESH LIME JUICE

¾ OZ / 22 ½ ML DEMERARA SUGAR
SYRUP *(SEE PAGE 150)*

Pour all the ingredients into an ice-filled
highball glass, fill it with crushed ice, and
swizzle (see page 56). Top with more crushed
ice and garnish with a sprig of fresh mint.

There's something magical about visiting the world's grand hotels and partaking in one of their signature cocktails, surrounded by the history of the iconic bar rooms in which they were created. Stepping over discarded peanut shells at the Long Bar in Singapore's Raffle's Hotel for a Singapore Sling; escaping the hedonism of New Orleans' Bourbon Street for a Vieux Carré at the Carousel Bar in the Hotel Monteleone; side-stepping the hustle and bustle of the Strand in London for a White Lady at the American Bar in the Savoy Hotel; or escaping the heat of Marrakech for a Churchill Martini at the Churchill Bar in La Mamounia. These institutions have done as much as any to keep cocktail culture alive throughout the decades.

Unfortunately, one such famed establishment, Port of Spain's Queen's Park Hotel, was torn down in 1996 to make way for offices for the BPTT oil company, thus removing the chance to enjoy their famed Queen's Park Swizzle. Described by Trader Vic in his *Book of Food & Drink* (1946) as *"the most delightful form of anesthesia given out today,"* the drink fortunately survives in bar-rooms across the globe. It's a potent combination of Demerara rum, fresh lime juice, mint leaves, sugar, and Angostura Bitters, and makes for a perfect hot-weather drink. It's lesser-known sibling, the Queen's Park Special, which I first found referenced in *Harper's Bazaar* from 1941, deserves more attention. Utilizing the lighter butterscotch, cocoa, and vanilla notes of Trinidadian rum, the introduction of Falernum adds a layer of sweetness, spice, and freshness, with the latter accentuated by the garnish, and of course the bitters, which add length and depth.

GIN PAHIT

Unknown origin

1 ½ OZ / 45 ML PLYMOUTH GIN
NAVY STRENGTH

½ OZ / 15 ML AROMATIC BITTERS
*(ANGOSTURA, THE BITTER
TRUTH OLD TIME, OR DR.
ADAM ELMEGIRAB'S ORINOCO
AROMATIC BITTERS)*

1 TEASPOON / 5 ML SUGAR SYRUP
(SEE PAGE 150)

*Add all the ingredients to a mixing vessel, fill
it with cubed ice, and briskly stir for around
15–20 seconds. Strain into a pre-chilled
cocktail glass and garnish with a coin of fresh
lemon zest and, optionally, onions pickled in
chili vinegar served on the side.*

If you've ever wondered how to say *"bitter gin"*
in Malay, now you know. In fact, it is the Gin
Pahit that is largely responsible for the success
of the Angostura Bitters brand. While serving
for Venezuelan military leader Simón Bolívar
in the port of Angostura, Dr. Johann Gottlieb
Benjamin Siegert seized the opportunity to
market his newly created bitters as a remedy
for seasickness for the many sailors who would
frequent the town. Quickly gaining in popularity
with the Royal Navy, it would not be long before
they started adding dashes of their new elixir
to their favorite Plymouth Gin, and so the Pink
Gin was born. It would later be the colonies in
British Malaya who would increase the ratio
of bitters for the Pahit, presumably as a way to
adjust their stomachs to their new climate.

Sugar is not a standard requirement in a classic
Pink Gin or Gin Pahit, but I've found it to be
preferable for those who are feeling adventurous
and/or testing the water. However, the hardened
drinkers among us who like their drinks with
more intensity may wish to get their lips around
the Gin Piaj, which keeps the three-to-one ratio,
sans sugar or lemon zest. This is also stirred
with ice but, to finish, skewer a couple of spiced
pickled onions and drop them in the drink. Hot,
spicy, and bracing, it's not for everyone, but
delightful to a few.

TUXEDO

Harry MacElhone, Harry's New York Bar, Paris, France

1 ½ OZ / 45 ML OLD TOM GIN

1 ½ OZ / 45 ML NOILLY PRAT DRY
VERMOUTH

3 DASHES ANGOSTURA
ORANGE BITTERS

1 DASH MARASCHINO
LIQUEUR

1 DASH ABSINTHE

Add all the ingredients to your mixing vessel, fill it with cubed ice, and briskly stir for around 15–20 seconds. Strain into a pre-chilled cocktail glass and garnish with a coin of lemon zest snapped over the drink and then discarded.

An hour south of my hometown of Aberdeen you'll find the city of Dundee, the home of one of the most influential figures in the history of bartending. Born on June 16, 1890, Harry MacElhone started his bar career working at Cinq Rue Daunou in Paris before heading to the US to work in Connecticut and New York and returning to Europe in 1914 to serve in the RAF during World War I. Following the end of the war, MacElhone resumed his bartending career, first with the Ciro's Club in London, then at their second outpost in Deauville, France. After securing the money to open his own bar, MacElhone would return to Paris in 1923 to open Harry's New York Bar. The address? Where it all began for Harry, Cinq Rue Daunou (*Sank Roo Doe Noo*), which is still owned and operated to this day by Harry's descendants.

Almost a century later his legacy lives on with creations such as the Monkey Gland, Between the Sheets, and White Lady. He is also famed for his 1927 tome *Barflies and Cocktails*, which offered a snapshot into life in Europe during the US Prohibition era when American bartenders were generally forced to leave their home country to pursue their bartending career. In this book, MacElhone also penned his phenomenal take on the Tuxedo cocktail. Fundamentally, it's a riff between the original Martini and Dry Martini, with sweet and dry ingredients crucial to its success; the additional sugar amplifies the flavor, while the accents of Maraschino, absinthe, and orange bitters bring the noise.

SWEET

———

Unquestionably the most desired of the five tastes, our craving for sweetness dates back millions of years to our prehistoric ancestors, as explained by Daniel Liebermann, paleoanthropologist at Harvard University, in *The New York Times* of June 5, 2012: *"Simply put, humans evolved to crave sugar, store it, and then use it. For millions of years, our cravings and digestive systems were exquisitely balanced because sugar was rare. Apart from honey, most of the foods our hunter-gatherer ancestors ate were no sweeter than a carrot. The invention of farming made starchy foods more abundant, but it wasn't until very recently that technology made pure sugar bountiful."*

If it is not used by the body straight away, sugar is stored as fat, which would have been a way to prevent starvation when sugar was scarce. Things are very different nowadays with sugar present in nearly everything we consume, from ketchup to flavored water. Additionally, the consumption of sugar activates the brain's reward system, releasing dopamine, which also occurs when we take drugs, socialize, and have sex.

Sugar's role in drinks is primarily as a flavor carrier, helping to build layers of flavor on our palates, while also counterbalancing bitter and sour flavors. This is best showcased when you add a dash of sweetness to stirred drinks which are generally quite dry; for example, a Martini with gin and vermouth will have its flavor heightened with the addition of a dash of sweet Orange Curaçao, Maraschino Liqueur, or honey.

NORDIC CLUB

Author's own

4 FRESH RASPBERRIES

1 ½ OZ / 45 ML GERANIUM GIN

½ OZ / 15 ML AALBORG TAFFEL AKVAVIT

1 DASH DR. ADAM ELMEGIRAB'S
  DANDELION & BURDOCK BITTERS

¾ OZ / 22 ½ ML FRESH LEMON JUICE

½ OZ / 15 ML SUGAR SYRUP (*SEE PAGE 150*)

½ OZ / 15 ML FRESH EGG WHITE

Add all the ingredients to a cocktail shaker, quickly dry-shake, then fill with cubed ice, and shake hard for 10 seconds. Strain into a pre-chilled cocktail glass.

Philadelphia's Bellevue-Stratford hotel—the place to be seen in the late 1800s—regularly played host to The Clover Club, an exclusive gentleman's group consisting of businessmen, writers, and lawyers who are also credited with creating a cocktail of the same name, comprising gin, dry vermouth, raspberry syrup, lemon juice, and egg white. It is this cocktail which inspired the adapted Nordic Club.

Native to Scandinavia, Akvavit is a flavored spirit distilled from potatoes or grain. Its predominant flavor is nutty, aromatic caraway, which is backed up by other botanicals such as lemon, star anise, fennel, dill, cloves, and cardamom, to name but a few. Used in scant quantities it offers similar properties to dry vermouth when offering balance to a drink. The formulas of the Clover and the Nordic Clubs are similar, but there is a more prevalent warming character in the latter, with the ginger, anise, and orange in Dandelion & Burdock Bitters working in tandem with the Akvavit to offer an autumnal quality.

AÑEJO HIGHBALL

*Dale DeGroff, Rainbow Room,
New York City, USA*

1 ½ oz / 45 ml AÑEJO RUM

½ oz / 15 ml PIERRE FERRAND
ORANGE CURAÇAO

½ oz / 15 ml FRESH LIME JUICE

2 oz / 60 ml GINGER BEER

2 DASHES DALE DEGROFF'S
PIMENTO AROMATIC
BITTERS

*Build all the ingredients in an ice-filled
highball glass, lightly stir, and garnish with
a slice each of fresh lime and fresh orange.*

Undoubtedly the most famous bartender living today, Rhode Island native Dale DeGroff is widely credited for helping kick-start the modern cocktail renaissance during his stint at New York City's Rainbow Room. Following seven years working in LA's Hotel Bel-Air from 1978, DeGroff was approached by famed restaurateur Joe Baum to oversee the bar at his New York restaurant Aurora. DeGroff was instructed by Baum to create "a classic 19th-century bar, and if you don't know how to do it, find a book called *How to Mix Drinks* by Jerry Thomas. It'll teach you how to do it. I don't want anything artificial. I don't want any guns, nothing like that. Splits of soda, fresh everything."

The challenge was set...

After two years at Aurora, DeGroff took his newfound knowledge and skill across to Baum's larger project—the Rainbow Room. It was there that DeGroff's career really took off and where the lost art of cocktail bartending began to grab the attention of the wider world. DeGroff's influence extends far and wide, with many of the world's influential bar owners and bartenders having worked alongside or trained under him, and I defy anyone to tell me they've never seen a strip of orange zest flamed over a Cosmopolitan at a bar somewhere. Yep, that was DeGroff's doing, too.

The Añejo Highball is unquestionably one of DeGroff's most well-known drinks, created in 1990 as a tribute to Cuban bartenders while he was consulting for Angostura Bitters. It wouldn't surprise me if his recipe was inspired by the Bermudan Dark 'N' Stormy, one of the few trademarked cocktails in the world, which calls for Gosling's dark rum, ginger beer, and fresh lime. DeGroff's interpretation focuses on the combination of toffee, coffee, and spice-rich Añejo rum, alongside sweet, spicy ginger beer and a little fresh lime juice to balance. While that may seem like an obvious pairing, it's the addition of Orange Curaçao—think notes of zesty orange, cinnamon, marmalade, and black pepper—which really elevates this serve and confirms DeGroff's genius. The bitters originally used were Angostura; however DeGroff has reimagined the recipe using his own outstanding Pimento Bitters (better known as allspice to some), which are packed full of baking spice flavors, namely clove, black pepper, cinnamon, anise, and ginger.

FOSBURY FLIP

Author's own

1 TEASPOON CARAWAY SEEDS

2 oz / 60 ML DRAMBUIE

1 oz / 30 ML BACARDI 8 AÑOS RUM

2 DASHES BITTERMENS
    XOCOLATL MOLE BITTERS

1 LARGE FREE-RANGE EGG

1 TEASPOON / 5 ML SUGAR SYRUP
    (*SEE PAGE 150*)

1 GRIND ROCK SALT

1 GRIND BLACK PEPPER

Muddle the caraway seeds in the base of a cocktail shaker, add the liquor, and steep for 2 minutes. Add the remaining ingredients, quickly dry-shake, then fill with cubed ice and shake hard for a further 10 seconds. Strain into a pre-chilled goblet, then garnish with a dusting of freshly grated nutmeg

The inspiration behind the Fosbury Flip came from reading about the life of American high-jumper Richard Douglas Fosbury, more commonly known as "Dick" Fosbury, while I researched for a cocktail competition in 2010. Fosbury revolutionized the high jump during the 1968 Olympic Games in Mexico City by utilizing his *back first* technique, which earned him the gold medal. His pioneering technique was fondly referred to as the "Fosbury Flop," a style of jump adopted nowadays by almost every high jumper in the world.

While preparing for athletic meets, Dick would consume vast quantities of protein by way of raw eggs, flavored with little more than pinches of salt and pepper. It also came to light that he would celebrate successful jump meets with a glass of Drambuie*, a Scotch whisky liqueur flavored with honey, herbs, and spices. Taking inspiration from this, it made sense to create a Flip in Dick's honor. Flips, as we know them nowadays, are a mix of whole raw eggs, spirit, sugar, and spices—if you must, a more elegant take on the festive Egg Nog which also includes cream. The combination of sweet and spicy Drambuie, the tropical and dried fruits in the rum, spiced chocolate bitters, and the accents of salt and pepper, all bound together in the beaten egg make for a truly wonderful take on a personal favorite family of drinks.

* DISCLAIMER: The story about Fosbury loving raw eggs and Drambuie I made up on the spot while waiting to present my drink at the competition. It was enough to help secure a win though.

FLORABOTANICA

Jason Williams, Proof & Co., Singapore

2 OZ / 60 ML THE WEST WINDS
THE SABRE GIN

½ OZ / 15 ML YUZU JUICE

½ OZ / 15 ML MONIN ROSE SYRUP

4 DASHES DR. ADAM
ELMEGIRAB'S DANDELION
& BURDOCK BITTERS

1 TEASPOON / 5 ML MARASCHINO
LIQUEUR

½ OZ / 15 ML FRESH EGG WHITE

*Add all the ingredients to a cocktail shaker,
quickly dry-shake, then fill with cubed ice
and shake hard for around 10 seconds. Strain
into an ice-filled rocks glass and garnish with
a dehydrated orange wheel and edible flowers.*

I can hear the shouts already, *"That's an
adaptation of a gin sour; it's not a sweet drink,"* and
I would be inclined to agree, especially as I'm
a known pedant, but let me explain. In their
original form, both the marasca cherry (a sour
Morello cherry which gives Maraschino liqueur
its distinct flavor) and rose petals are not sweet
in any way, shape, or form. However, as they've
both been used for centuries to flavor sugar-
rich food and beverages, we assume they'll taste
sweet. The same can be said of the likes of
vanilla and cacao, which are actually inherently
bitter, or of cranberries, which are typically used
in sweetened jellies, jams, and juices to reduce
their tartness.

In the Florabotanica, the addition of sweet
rose syrup and dry cherry liqueur are put to
great effect to balance the classically inspired
The West Winds The Sabre Gin, and the yuzu
juice, an incredibly sour and fragrant citrus fruit
which is primarily cultivated in Korea, Japan,
and China. The licorice flavor in the bitters,
thanks to star anise, comes to the fore at the
finish, with a rich mouthfeel present throughout
thanks to the egg white.

TREACLE

Dick Bradsell, El Camion, London, UK

2 OZ / 60 ML GOSLING'S BLACK
SEAL RUM

2 DASHES ANGOSTURA
BITTERS

½ OZ / 15 ML SUGAR SYRUP
(SEE PAGE 150)

½ OZ / 15 ML FRESHLY PRESSED
APPLE JUICE

Add the first three ingredients to a mixing vessel, fill it with cubed ice, and briskly stir for around 15–20 seconds. Strain into an ice-filled rocks glass, top with the apple juice, and garnish with a coin of fresh orange zest snapped over and dropped into the drink.

I'd say it's fair to assume that it's the dream of most bartenders to create a cocktail which, at some point in time, will be viewed as a classic, a feat Bradsell has achieved countless times. There's no magic formula to follow, should anyone wish to know how he did it, because numerous factors are involved, but his skill in taking a tried-and-tested drink's formula and introducing a point of difference to elevate it was enviable. For the Bramble you have a simple Gin Sour (*gin, lemon, sugar*) finished with blackberry liqueur. The Russian Spring Punch is a Raspberry Collins (*vodka, lemon, raspberry, sugar, soda*) with Champagne taking the place of soda and adding a layer of elegance. And in this case the Treacle is a Rum Old Fashioned (*rum, bitters, sugar*) crowned with freshly pressed apple juice. The combination of flavors gives you a drink that tastes like… well, the clue is in the name. It's just delicious.

THE MAN WHO MADE CLASSICS

It would be remiss of me to write a book covering the history of cocktails and not mention Dick Bradsell. You may not have heard of him, or been fortunate enough to frequent one of his bars, but I can almost guarantee you've either (a) had one of the many contemporary classics created by him: The Bramble, the Polish Martini, the Snood Murdekin, the Russian Spring Punch, the Vodka Espresso (*aka the Espresso Martini*), the Wibble, or the Treacle, (b) have been served by a bartender directly trained by Bradsell, or (c) been served by a Bradsell disciple. Where the USA had Dale Degroff (*see the Añejo Highball, page 88*), the UK had Dick Bradsell. His impact on bartending cannot be overstated. Sadly Dick passed away at the age of 56 in 2016, but his legend will live on. I hope everyone that reads this will take the opportunity to make it for themselves, and when they do, raise the glass to Dick and all those closest to your heart. "*Cheers.*"

CHAMPAGNE COCKTAIL

Unknown origin

1 BROWN SUGAR CUBE

3 DASHES PEYCHAUD'S
    BITTERS

½ OZ / 15 ML VSOP COGNAC
    (OPTIONAL)

4 OZ / 120 ML CHAMPAGNE

Place the sugar cube on a spoon, dash the bitters onto it, then drop it in the base of a Champagne flute. Add the Cognac, then top with the Champagne. Garnish with a spiral of fresh lemon zest.

First surfacing in San Francisco in 1850, 44 years after our first written cocktail definition from *The Balance and Columbian Repository (see page 15)*, the Champagne Cocktail marks the start of "cocktail" becoming a catch-all term. For fact's sake (don't say that loudly after a few drinks), it should be noted that the earliest references did include ice but I would skip that step.

For this recipe I've included my preferred serve for a Champagne Cocktail, with the inclusion of Cognac. This style was popularized in the UK and was taught to me as being *"the London way,"* having first surfaced in the *Café Royal Cocktail Book*, a publication produced by the United Kingdom Bartender's Guild in 1937. The combination of bitters and sugar does as you'd expect, adding depth and balance to the drink, while the Champagne offers elegant effervescence and the Cognac adds that bit extra with hints of dried fruit, vanilla, nuts, and spice. Should you wish for some additional fruity sweetness, you could swap out the Cognac for an Orange Curaçao or Apricot Brandy. If you're wanting a big boozy hit, drop the sugar, bitters, and Cognac altogether and turn it up to 11 with Ernest Hemingway's *Death in the Afternoon*, as described in the 1935 publication *So Red the Nose*, a collection of recipes submitted by celebrated authors of the time. The method goes: *"Pour one jigger of absinthe into a Champagne glass. Add iced Champagne until it attains the proper opalescent milkiness. Drink 3 to 5 of these slowly."*

EAST INDIA COCKTAIL

Unknown origin

2 OZ / 60 ML VSOP COGNAC

1 TEASPOON / 5 ML ORANGE
   CURAÇAO

3 DASHES DR. ADAM
   ELMEGIRAB'S BOKER'S
   BITTERS OR ANGOSTURA
   BITTERS

2 DASHES MARASCHINO
   LIQUEUR

1 TEASPOON / 5 ML PINEAPPLE
   SYRUP (*SEE PAGE 151*)

Add all the ingredients to a cocktail shaker, fill it with cubed ice, and shake hard for around 10 seconds. Strain into a pre-chilled cocktail glass and garnish with a coin of fresh lemon zest or a cocktail cherry.

The East India Cocktail is another great example of the continued evolution of the cocktail throughout the 19th century. Going beyond the Brandy Crusta (*see page 61*), with its addition of lemon juice and elaborate garnish, the East India marks the introduction of exotic ingredients with the inclusion of pineapple (*see the Chelsea Dove, page 105*). The above recipe would feature in Harry Johnson's *New and Improved Bartender's Manual* of 1888, six years after the first edition was published, which strangely included the exact same drink but with raspberry syrup in place of pineapple. It is widely agreed that the pineapple variant produces a superior beverage, which may explain why Johnson amended the recipe. Other than that little is given away apart from his footnote that *"This drink is a great favorite with the English living in the different parts of East India."*

In relation to which bitters to use in this drink, Angostura first appeared in 1882, Boker's in 1888. The baking spice notes of Angostura are a great accompaniment to raspberry syrup, while Boker's, with their notes of orange, smoked tea, cardamom, and coffee, work wonderfully well with pineapple and Cognac.

AN INTERESTING ASIDE

In 1900, Harry Johnson claimed that he originally published 10,000 copies of his
bartender's manual in 1860 while working in San Francisco, preceding Jerry
Thomas's seminal *Bartender's Guide* from 1862. To this day, no such copy of a book by
Johnson has surfaced.

MONTANA

Unknown origin

1 ½ OZ / 45 ML SLOE GIN

1 ½ OZ / 45 ML NOILLY PRAT DRY
VERMOUTH

3 DASHES ANISETTE (*ARAK,
OUZO, OR RAKI*)

3 DASHES SCRAPPY'S
CARDAMOM BITTERS

Add all the ingredients to your mixing vessel, fill it with cubed ice, and briskly stir for around 15–20 seconds. Strain into a pre-chilled cocktail glass.

St. Germain elderflower liqueur is often referred to as *bartender's ketchup*, being the first liqueur that truly bridged the gap between 1990s disco drinks (think Peach Schnapps or Blue Curaçao) and the modern craft cocktail movement, working magnificently well when added to any sour, punch, cocktail, or fizz. By creating a subtly sweet liqueur packed full of balanced floral and fruity notes, the sadly departed Rob Cooper left an indelible mark on the drinks industry. Jump back a few decades and apricot brandy, for me THE most underrated product in the world of cocktails, had a similar impact following on from the early successes of the original *ketchups*, orange Curaçao and Maraschino Liqueur.

Sloe gin is another bottling I've always felt has been overlooked. Fuller than St. Germain, it ultimately has a similar profile with rich fruity (*berry, cherry, and citrus*) and floral notes being prevalent. Its added body allows it to stand up as a base spirit, but its sweetness and complexity ensures it doubles up as an outstanding modifier. In the Montana, as found in the 1900 edition of Harry Johnson's *New & Improved Bartender's Manual*, sloe gin shares center stage with dry vermouth, while the aniseed and licorice flavors in the anisette and the citrus, perfumed, and menthol notes of green cardamom offer the crucial flavor accents required for balance. I always list this drink whenever I work the occasional bartending shift, and it regularly features at branded training sessions. To this day I've yet to find one person who didn't fall in love with this drink.

ABOUKIR PUNCH

Joseph Akhavan, Mabel, Paris, France

2 oz / 60 ml PANDAN-INFUSED
    TAWNY PORT (*SEE PAGE 155*)

1 oz / 30 ml DOORLY'S 5-YEAR-
    OLD RUM

1 oz / 30 ml GRAPEFRUIT &
    CARDAMOM SHERBET
    (*SEE PAGE 154*)

3 DASHES DR. ADAM
    ELMEGIRAB'S TEAPOT
    BITTERS

Build all the ingredients in an ice-filled highball glass, fill it with crushed ice, and swizzle (see page 56). Top with more crushed ice and garnish with pan masala (also known as paan) and a sprig of fresh mint.

It's widely believed that punches were discovered by British colonists in India sometime during the 16th century. The name "punch" is derived from the Indian word for "five," *panch*, and is believed to refer to the five constituent ingredients: arrack, sugar, lemons, water, and tea. As with most stories surrounding mixed beverages, this has many variations, which is not surprising as there's rarely someone present who is sober enough to keep track of things. Whatever the truth regarding the exact origins of punch, there is solid evidence that it traveled with English colonists who relocated from India to the New World, with references to it dating as far back as 1682. One such reference from 1757 is attributed to an *"S.M of Boston,"* believed to be Samuel Mather, the son of Cotton Mather, a minister from New England. Mather sent a box of lemons to his friend Sir Harry Frankland along with the following verse:

*"You know from Eastern India came
The skill of making punch as did the name.
And as the name consists of letters five,
By five ingredients it is kept alive.
To purest water sugar must be joined,
With these the grateful acid is combined.
Some any sours they get contented use,
But men of taste do that from Tagus choose.
When now these three are mixed with care
Then added be of spirit a small share.
And that you may the drink quite perfect see,
Atop the musky nut must grated be."*

The Aboukir Punch is a modern adaptation that stays fairly true to the original *panch* ingredients; the arrack is replaced with rum, the sugar and lemon with grapefruit sherbet, the water with ice, and tea is found in the infused bitters. Spices such as nutmeg, cinnamon, and cardamom have also long been utilized in punch recipes, and here they are represented both in the bitters and through the cardamom in the sherbet. The real star in this show, though, is the pandan, with its fragrant, vanilla, and sweet grassy notes proving to be an ideal partner for the woody, dark-fruit flavors of the Tawny port.

HANKY SPANKY

Jack Forbes, Cloakroom Bar,
Montreal, Canada

1 ½ oz / 45 ml OLD RAJ GIN

1 ½ oz / 45 ml COCCHI VERMOUTH
    DI TORINO

1 TEASPOON / 5 ml DR. ADAM
    ELMEGIRAB'S APHRODITE
    BITTERS

3 DASHES FERNET BRANCA,
    TO RINSE

Add the first three ingredients to a mixing
vessel, fill it with cubed ice, and briskly stir
for around 15–20 seconds. Strain into a pre-
chilled cocktail glass which has been rinsed
with the Fernet Branca. Garnish with a
cocktail cherry.

Arguably the world's most iconic cocktail venue, the American Bar at the Savoy Hotel opened in 1889. Since they first swung open their doors, the bar has had just 11 head bartenders overseeing operations: Frank Wells, Ruth Burgess, Ada Coleman, Eddie Clark, Reginald Johnson, Joe Gilmore, Harry Viccars, Victor Gower, Peter Dorelli, Salim Khoury, and Erik Lorincz. Ada "Coley" Coleman's stint at the Savoy began in 1899. *"I remember it was a Manhattan that I made first, and that it was Fisher, the wine butler, who gave me my first lesson,"* she would later recall in an interview with the *Daily Express* in 1925. The interview was to announce her retirement following a 23-year reign as head bartender after taking the role in 1903.

The only drink credited to Coleman in Harry Craddock's 1930 *Savoy Cocktail Book*, the Hanky Panky is said to have gained its name after she created it for English actor Charles Hawtrey. Recalling the drink's creation, Coleman said, *"Some years ago, when [Hawtrey] was over-working, he used to come into the bar and say 'Coley, I am tired. Give me something with a bit of punch in it.'"* Combining dry gin, sweet vermouth, and the Italian amaro Fernet Branca, Coleman would hand it over to Hawtrey, who would quickly drain the glass before exclaiming, *"By Jove! That is the real hanky-panky!"*

The Hanky Spanky doesn't stray too far away from Coleman's original, but introduces deeper notes of dark fruits, cacao, coffee, chocolate, and warm spices, thanks to the vermouth, bitters, and spicy gin, while the Fernet's role is for its aromatic properties which add a fragrant, menthol note on the nose.

SALT

———

Despite its links to heart attacks, strokes, and high blood pressure in people who consume too much of it, salt is required by the human body and, as such, it is an essential part of our diets. Consisting of two electrolytes, sodium and chloride (hence its scientific name sodium chloride), salt helps maintain fluid balance, which determines blood volume and in turn regulates blood pressure; generates nerve impulses; and helps the intestines absorb nutrients, including amino acids, chloride, glucose, and water. Unlike vitamins and minerals such as Vitamin D and calcium, which are stored in the body to be used as required, we can't keep reserves of salt so, when we come across it, it's beneficial to eat it which goes some way to explain why we crave it so much.

In the world of food and drink, salt is something of an antithesis to bitterness, because it suppresses bitter flavors. However, much like the way bitters work, it improves the overall taste of what it comes into contact with by heightening the flavor intensity. Salt will hide chemical or metallic off-notes and, by tempering bitterness, it enhances sweetness and makes sour flavors appear brighter. This is why bartenders often have a bottle of saline solution (10 parts water to 1 part salt) at hand, to add a few dashes to sour heavy drinks such as a Collins or Daiquiri. Saline Solution (*see page 155*) is especially handy to give life to freshly squeezed citrus when it's not produced to order; a few drops added to bitter drinks such as the Negroni will increase the citrus flavor and the sweetness of the Campari and vermouth. Salt has often been overlooked in the world of mixed drinks but it has earned a seat at the top table. In the right hands, it is an essential ingredient.

CHELSEA DOVE

Author's own

2 oz / 60 ml TANQUERAY GIN

4 DASHES DR. ADAM ELMEGIRAB'S
TEAPOT BITTERS

4 oz / 120 ml PINEAPPLE SODA

½ oz / 15 ml LEMON SHERBET (*SEE PAGE 153*)

PINCH VANILLA SALT (*SEE PAGE 155*)

Build all the ingredients in an ice-filled highball glass, lightly stir, and garnish with two pineapple fronds.

La Paloma was thought to have been created by Don Javier Delgado Corona of the renowned bar La Capilla, in Tequila, Mexico. The cocktail has gained a cult following in recent years along with the growing interest in tequila and mezcal. A simple beverage consisting of blanco tequila, grapefruit soda, lime juice, and salt, there are few drinks as refreshing as the Paloma with its crisp bite of two citrus fruits playing wonderfully alongside the earthy, spicy tequila. Finally, a hint of salt heightens the flavor and adds to its mouthwatering qualities.

My version utilizes juniper-heavy London Dry Gin and I settled on pineapple soda as the lengthener, having been drawn to the pineapple crest on bottles of Tanqueray gin. Pineapple has long been a symbol that represents hospitality and success, and was a sign of wealth in the 19th century. The flavor profile of Tanqueray, with pine, lemon, coriander, and floral notes, works in harmony with the sweet soda. To cut through this mixture, I added the Lemon Sherbet (produced by combining lemon peel with sugar to extract the essential oils, then dissolving the sugar in lemon juice) and Vanilla Salt to add fragrance and accentuate the flavors. I added the bitters not necessarily for bitterness, but instead to offer tea and spice notes to round off an invigorating long drink.

LADY COLOMBIA

Alex Lawrence, Dandelyan, London, UK

2 oz / 60 ml LA HECHICERA RUM

¾ oz / 22 ½ ml MARTINI EXTRA DRY VERMOUTH

1 TEASPOON / 5 ml MOZART DARK CHOCOLATE LIQUEUR

1 TEASPOON / 5 ml MAPLE SYRUP

1 DASH DR. ADAM ELMEGIRAB'S APHRODITE BITTERS

1 DASH DR. ADAM ELMEGIRAB'S ORINOCO AROMATIC BITTERS

PINCH OF SEA SALT

Add all the ingredients to a mixing vessel, fill it with cubed ice, and briskly stir for around 15–20 seconds. Strain into an ice-filled rocks glass and garnish with a coin of fresh lemon zest snapped over and dropped into the drink.

Resembling a hybrid of the Old Fashioned (*spirit, sugar, water, and bitters*) and Palmetto (*rum, vermouth, and bitters*), the Lady Colombia was created by London-based bartender Alex Lawrence, then of Orchid in my hometown of Aberdeen. and was the winning drink from the 2014 La Hechicera cocktail challenge that took him to Colombia for a month-long stint representing the brand in Bogota and Cartagena. With the complex rum at its base, sporting a myriad of flavors, from chocolate to toffee, and black pepper to vanilla, the dry, floral vermouth provides a perfect backdrop and complements the rich sweeteners in the liqueur and maple syrup. The cocktail is seasoned with the cacao- and coffee-based Aphrodite Bitters (another nod to Colombia), while the warm, aromatic Orinoco Bitters brings everything together, but the hint of salt is genius, making all the flavors burst in tandem while adding a touch of elegance.

A NEW COLOMBIAN EXPORT

More famous for its excellent coffee, diverse selection of exotic fruits, emeralds, and beautiful women, Colombia is also making its mark in the world of rum. The likes of Dictador, Ron Medellin, and specifically in this case, La Hechicera, a blend of 12–21-year-old rums produced by the Riasco family in Barranquilla, Northern Colombia, using the Solera process commonly adopted in the production of fortified wines, beers, and Balsamic vinegars.

A BEER AND A SMOKE

Jim Meehan, PDT, New York, USA

1 OZ / 30 ML SOMBRA MEZCAL

¾ OZ / 22 ½ ML FRESH LIME JUICE

4 DASHES CHOLULA HOT
    SAUCE

1 DASH BITTER TRUTH
    CELERY BITTERS

6 OZ / 180 ML PILSNER BEER

KOSHER SALT, CELERY SALT,
    & SUGAR MIX (*FOR RIM,
    SEE PAGE 155*)

Add the first four ingredients to a mixing vessel, fill it with cubed ice, and briskly stir for around 15–20 seconds. Strain into a highball glass which has been rimmed with the Kosher Salt, Celery Salt, & Sugar Mix, top with the chilled beer, and garnish with freshly grated orange and lime zest.

Any bartender worth their salt, pun intended, will swear by the restorative properties of the Bloody Mary or Red Snapper after a heavy night's drinking. However, you shouldn't be surprised to find another collective that swears by the benefits of the *Cerveza preparada*, a catch-all term in Mexico to describe beer mixed with tomato juice, hot sauce, and other flavorings. Its most well-known variant is the Michelada, a delicious combination usually consisting of beer, tomato juice, fresh lime juice, hot sauce, spices, and salt. As with the Bloody Mary, the perfect recipe is in the eye of the beholder with the only common ingredient being a light crisp lager of the Pilsner style.

A Beer and a Smoke is a heady take on the Michelada and was created by PDT bar owner Jim Meehan in the spring of 2009. This adaptation does not include tomato or Clamato juice, instead focusing on the citrus flavors found within. This offers up a more refined beverage that is complemented and tempered by the salt and sugar combination and the vegetal, savory, and herbaceous Celery Bitters, which offer further spice and work as a perfect partner for the smoky mezcal. Meehan recommends 4 dashes of the hot sauce, but those who favor spicy foods, like myself, may be tempted to add another few dashes. To finish, the grating of fresh citrus zest is a masterstroke that adds further depth and complexity along with incredible aromatics on the nose.

MEXICAN "FIRING SQUAD" SPECIAL

Unknown, La Cucaracha, Mexico City, Mexico

1 ½ OZ / 45 ML OCHO BLANCO
   TEQUILA

¾ OZ / 22 ½ ML FRESH LIME JUICE

½ OZ / 15 ML GRENADINE

2 DASHES ANGOSTURA
   BITTERS

3 DASHES SALINE SOLUTION
   (*SEE PAGE 155*)

Add all the ingredients to a cocktail shaker, fill it with cubed ice, and shake hard for around 10 seconds. Strain into an ice-filled rocks glass, and garnish with a lime wedge and also a cherry.

Much of the history of mixed drinks is open to debate for the fundamental reason that very few people document what's happening when many drinks are being consumed; just think about it, we've all had that bleary feeling of not remembering what happened the night before, or at least try our best not to! Thanks to the likes of well-traveled author Charles H. Baker, who did document his findings in his 1939 *Gentleman's Companion*, his 1946 editions of the same name (which included a food and drinks book), and the 1951 *South American Gentleman's Companion*, we

have a relatively solid time-stamp for drinks of the period. I say relatively because Baker was known to enjoy a tipple or three, citing Ernest Hemingway as an example of one of his confidantes.

Discovered in 1937, Baker recalled the *Mexican "Firing Squad" Special* in his 1939 tome as *"a creation we almost became wrecked upon in—of all spots—La Cucaracha Bar in Mexico City."* The combination is nothing overly creative; it's simplistic and closely related to the sour, rickey, and daisy families of drinks, but as a combination it's nothing short of delightful. Baker's recipe was simply two parts of tequila to one of fresh lime juice, grenadine, or gomme syrup to sweeten and aromatic bitters to finish. I've adjusted the recipe slightly to increase the sour element for modern tastes. The bitters pair perfectly with the tequila in pulling out the warm spices like black pepper and cinnamon that you expect to find, while the grenadine enhances and complements the fruitiness of the spirit. To elevate things further, a few dashes of Saline Solution really take the flavor up a notch, while also making for a richer mouthfeel. Some modern recipes also include soda water to create a fizz-style variant, although I'll leave it up to you to decide if that's desirable.

CELERY GIMLET

Naren Young, Dante, New York City, USA

1 ½ OZ / 45 ML TANQUERAY GIN

¼ OZ / 7 ½ ML GREEN CHARTREUSE

¼ OZ / 7 ½ ML ST. GERMAIN
ELDERFLOWER LIQUEUR

¾ OZ / 22 ½ ML FRESH LIME JUICE

½ OZ / 15 ML SUGAR SYRUP
(*SEE PAGE 150*)

½ OZ / 15 ML FRESH CELERY JUICE

5 DASHES WHITE WINE
VINEGAR

2 DASHES BITTER TRUTH
CELERY BITTERS

PINCH OF MALDON SALT

Add all the ingredients to a cocktail shaker, fill it with cubed ice, and shake hard for around 10 seconds. Strain into an ice-filled rocks glass and garnish with a ribbon of celery peeled using a potato peeler.

To combat scurvy, a disease resulting from a lack of Vitamin C, the 1867 *Merchant Shipping Act* made it compulsory that all ships in the British Navy carried stocks of lemon or lime juice, preserved with rum, to be dished out to sailors during voyages. This citrus juice was often mixed with sugar and routinely combined with water and the rum rations of sailors to create the drink we now know as Grog. It's also believed that naval officers would mix their lime juice with gin, which, after Scottish shipyard owner Lauchlan Rose patented a process to preserve lime juice with sugar to create his Rose's Lime Cordial, would ultimately lead to the formulation of the beverage we now know as the Gimlet. This drink, made with equal parts gin and lime cordial, has the makings of an incredibly quaffable drink. Sadly, Rose's Lime Cordial is now a shadow of its former self, but this has inspired many people to develop their own fresh lime cordial. Others went one step farther and stripped the Gimlet right back to the start, as showcased by Naren Young of Dante in New York. His Celery Gimlet combines a host of bartender favorites such as Chartreuse, Elderflower Liqueur, Celery Bitters, and white wine vinegar, culminating in a supremely refreshing Gimlet packed full of bright fresh herbal and vegetal flavors, with the salt again elevating all the ingredients as the perfect seasoning to this incredible cocktail.

SOUR

———

Probably the least understood of our five primary tastes, sourness is found in acidic foods containing organic acids such as malic (*apples and pears*), citric (*lemons, limes, and oranges*), and ascorbic (*peppers, tomatoes, and broccoli*). You will likely better know ascorbic acid as Vitamin C, an essential nutrient responsible for the repair and growth of tissue in all parts of the human body. This actually goes some way to explaining the difference between essential nutrients, those we have to introduce to our diets which also include proteins, fats, and carbohydrates, and non-essential nutrients, those which don't need worrying about as in some cases they are synthesized by the body. In this instance, if you don't consume enough Vitamin C you will develop scurvy, which can kill you.

Citrus fruits are a key ingredient in some of the world's most famous drinks such as the Daiquiri, White Lady, Whisk(e)y Sour, and Margarita. Though many fruits already contain a perfect combination of sugar and acid, hence the reason you can eat them in their natural state, lemons and limes contain lower levels of fructose and are thus favored in mixed drinks to counterbalance sweetness. This is why you'll see more recipes with fresh lemon and lime juice in comparison to say, orange, though a handy tip for any cocktail containing fresh orange juice is to add a few dashes of lemon to enliven the drink. Another tip for sour drinks is to add a few dashes of Saline Solution *(see page 155)* which again will brighten the drink and make the flavors "pop." Although it varies, sourness will temper the sensation of bitterness, letting the other flavors in bitters shine through.

LONDON CALLING

Chris Jepson, MadFox, Amsterdam, The Netherlands

1 ½ OZ / 45 ML BEEFEATER GIN

½ OZ / 15 ML FINO SHERRY

3 DASHES DR. ADAM ELMEGIRAB'S SPANISH BITTERS OR ORANGE BITTERS

½ OZ / 15 ML FRESH LEMON JUICE

½ OZ / 15 ML SUGAR SYRUP *(SEE PAGE 150)*

Add all the ingredients to a cocktail shaker, fill it with cubed ice, and shake hard for around 10 seconds. Strain into a pre-chilled cocktail glass and garnish with a coin of fresh grapefruit zest, snapped over and then dropped into the drink.

Popular with the bartending fraternity, particularly in its hometown of London, the London Calling has gained wider renown in recent years. This coincides with the growing interest in fortified wine, in this case sherry, as well as the explosion of gin in the last few years. The renaissance of cocktail culture is partly responsible for the world's developing enthusiasm for gin because it is likely the most popular spirit used in mixed drinks throughout history.

Created in 2002 by Chris Jepson, then of London's Milk & Honey, the London Calling bridges the gap between classical and modern cocktail movements. The drink is perfectly balanced, with the fruit and nut notes of the sherry complementing the orange and spice notes offered up by the gin. Originally it was created with an Orange Bitters, but I substitute this for Spanish Bitters, which shares four botanicals with the gin: angelica root, orange peel, coriander seed, and orris root, thus heightening and lengthening the flavor and in turn letting the base spirit shine.

SOUR

115

ARMY & NAVY

*Carroll Van Ark, PR Consultant,
New York, USA*

2 OZ / 60 ML BEEFEATER GIN

2 DASHES DR. ADAM
ELMEGIRAB'S BOKER'S
BITTERS

½ OZ / 15 ML FRESH LEMON JUICE

¼ OZ / 7 ½ ML ORGEAT SYRUP

Add all the ingredients to a cocktail shaker, fill it with cubed ice, and shake hard for around 10 seconds. Strain into a pre-chilled cocktail glass and garnish with fresh lemon zest, snapped over the drink and then discarded.

Ask any bartender about the Army & Navy and they'll likely reference David A. Embury, an American lawyer and cocktail aficionado who authored the outstanding *Fine Art of Mixing Drinks*, published in 1948. Embury championed his preferred 1-2-8 ratio for sour cocktails as left, which I agree makes a superior beverage. By contrast, the original called for two parts of gin to one part each of lemon and orgeat, making it overly sweet (the antithesis of what a sour drink should be), which also masks the flavor of the base spirit.

I called on famed historian Dave Wondrich to help uncover the cocktail's origin (seeing as Embury did not take credit for it), and discovered an earlier reference from 1937 by G. Selmer Fougner, America's first drinks writer. Fougner became best known for his *"Along the Wine Trail"* column in New York newspaper *The Sun*, which gained popularity following the repeal of Prohibition in the US in 1933. Fougner himself credited the drink's invention to "PR guy" Carroll Van Ark, father of American actress Joan Van Ark. Exactly when the drink was created is anyone's guess, although as Mr. Van Ark was born in 1897 and Prohibition ran from 1920 until 1933 I would hazard a guess at some time between 1933 and 1937. The drink was essentially a simple adaptation of a Gin Sour, replacing the sugar with almond syrup to give it a fragrant, nutty character. The inclusion of bitters is a relatively modern adaptation that makes the ingredients meld together even further, adding to the complexity of the drink.

VANILLA & COCONUT LASSI

Author's own

2 OZ / 60 ML BELVEDERE VODKA
(OR GREY GOOSE)

3 DASHES DR. ADAM
ELMEGIRAB'S TEAPOT
BITTERS

2 ½ OZ / 75 ML COCONUT MILK

1 OZ / 30 ML GREEK YOGURT

1 OZ / 30 ML VANILLA SUGAR
SYRUP *(SEE PAGE 151)*

1 OZ / 30 ML FRESH LIME JUICE

PINCH OF SAFFRON THREADS

PINCH OF GROUND
CARDAMOM

Add all the ingredients to a cocktail shaker and stir thoroughly to combine before filling it with cubed ice and shaking hard for around 10 seconds. Strain into an ice-filled highball glass and garnish with a pinch of saffron threads and ground cardamom.

As a lifelong lover of spicy foods, having been brought up by a Middle Eastern father, finding suitable drinks to pair with curries has always been an enjoyable challenge. A pint of Indian Kingfisher or Cobra lager, or more commonly a large G&T, are my typical go-to choices. However, a good lassi can perfectly offset hot spices, making it an even better accompaniment to a spicy curry than a lager. The refreshing, sour, subtly sweet, and cooling ingredients in a lassi make it an ideal warm-weather drink. This recipe was developed for an Indian restaurant I previously worked for. The savory, nutty, and fragrant vanilla and coconut hint at inherent sweetness, but these flavors are balanced superbly against the sour lime, yogurt, and array of spices, offering up an incredibly refreshing and moreish drink.

LASSI EXPLAINED

Lassi originated in the Indian subcontinent and is traditionally a savory beverage based around yogurt, water, and spices, although modifications on either side of the sweet and salty spectrum also exist. Regional variants can be found all over India calling for an array of unique ingredients such as butter to create a milkshake-style serve, fruits to cater for those with a sweet tooth, spices to enhance the classic savory offering, and herbs such as mint, as found in the salted mint lassi, which is popular in Bangladesh.

PISCO SOUR

Unknown origin

2 OZ / 60 ML MACCHU PISCO

1 OZ / 30 ML FRESH LEMON JUICE

½ OZ / 15 ML SUGAR SYRUP
  (SEE PAGE 150)

½ OZ / 15 ML FRESH EGG WHITE

3 DASHES AMARGO CHUNCHO
  BITTERS

Add the first four ingredients to a cocktail shaker, fill it with cubed ice, and shake hard for around 10 seconds. Strain into a pre-chilled cocktail glass and garnish with the dashes of bitters dropped into the foam of the egg white.

Born in Salt Lake City, Utah, in 1873, Victor Morris was an American bartender widely credited with creating the Pisco Sour, the national drink of Peru. At the age of 30, Morris moved from the US to Peru to work for the Cerro de Pasco railway company and would later move to the country's capital, Lima, in 1915, where he opened Morris Bar a year later. While there is no doubt Morris helped popularize the Pisco Sour, the Peruvian cookbook *Nuevo Manual de Cocina a la Criolla* from 1903 hinted at the drink having been around for a century. While the book simply calls it a cocktail, *sans* bitters of course, there can be little argument that this is a recipe for a Pisco Sour and that it had been around in Creole cuisine for some time.

The true origins of Pisco, a type of brandy distilled from grapes, have long been debated, with both Chile and Peru laying claim to it, but in this instance all the evidence provided suggests the Pisco Sour is a Peruvian drink; therefore I have called for a Peruvian Pisco and Peruvian bitters in this recipe. The Pisco is primarily centered around citrus, white pepper, vanilla, and grassy notes, a wonderful base from which to add the simple sour combination of lemon and sugar. The addition of egg white tempers the bite of citrus but compensates by adding incredible mouthfeel and texture. When the drink is shaken, the foam of the egg white offers a pillow on which you lay the bitters. Amargo (meaning bitter) Chuncho offers up the common baking spice associated with this Peruvian style of bitters, but also adds a cherry cola-like flavor and aroma unmistakable in the finish of this classic drink.

THE ORIGINAL?

Here is the recipe for the Pisco cocktail, as written in *Nuevo Manual de Cocina a la Criolla*:
"An egg white, a glass of pisco, a teaspoon of fine sugar, and a few drops of lemon at will, will open a good appetite.

Up to three glasses you can make with an egg white and a spoonful well filled with fine sugar, adding a little more for each glass. All this is beaten in a cocktail shaker or punch bowl, until forming a little punch."

DOWNRIVER

Liam Broom, Callooh Callay, London, UK

1 oz / 30 ml JASMINE
TEA-INFUSED VODKA
(SEE PAGE 154)

¾ oz / 22 ½ ml COCCHI
AMERICANO

1 oz / 30 ml HONEYDEW MELON
JUICE

¾ oz / 22 ½ ml LEMON JUICE

⅓ oz / 10 ml SUGAR SYRUP
(SEE PAGE 150)

2 DASHES DR. ADAM
ELMEGIRAB'S DANDELION
& BURDOCK BITTERS

SODA/SPARKLING WATER,
TO TOP UP

Add the first six ingredients to a cocktail shaker, fill it with cubed ice, and shake hard for around 10 seconds. Prior to straining, add a splash of soda water to your tin, then strain into an ice-filled highball glass. Garnish with two melon balls.

One of my favorite quotes is: *"In life it's never about the drink you're having, but what's happening around you when you're having that drink,"* and I truly believe that transfers across to all our drinking and dining experiences. In fact, I'm willing to bet that if I asked anyone reading this to recall their favorite meal or cocktail, I can almost guarantee they'll first talk about the company they were in, the weather on the day, the setting, or the music, with the actual dish or beverage an afterthought. That isn't to say they're not important, as the greatest bars and restaurants of the world demonstrate by pulling all those elements together.

It is this idea of the flavors and aromas found within food and drink triggering our favorite memories and experiences which is partly responsible for the inclusion of the Downriver. That crisp hit of fresh honeydew melon takes me back to a hot summer's day in Ibiza lying on the beach with my fiancée, or to a friend's barbecue during our annual seven days of Scottish summer. It's a wondrous experience we've all had at some point in our lives and I defy anyone to tell me otherwise, much like I defy anyone to go to Callooh Callay in London and not have fun. Just try not to forget what you had to drink.

SOUR

123

PENDENNIS CLUB COCKTAIL

Unknown origin

2 oz / 60 ml TANQUERAY GIN

1 oz / 30 ml APRICOT BRANDY

¾ oz / 22 ½ ml FRESH LIME JUICE

2 DASHES PEYCHAUD'S
    BITTERS

Add all the ingredients to a cocktail shaker, fill with cubed ice, and shake hard for around 10 seconds. Strain into a pre-chilled cocktail glass and garnish with a cocktail cherry.

First established in Louisville, Kentucky, in 1881, the Pendennis Club has earned global renown in the world of cocktails for the venue's claim to be the birthplace of the Old Fashioned. It does not claim to have invented the drink (it had been around long before), but rather it claims to be the venue where patrons of the bar first requested the "Old Fashioned" cocktail of spirit, sugar, water, and bitters *(see page 15)* by name. In the case of the Pendennis Club the spirit of choice was bourbon, much like it is the go-to for bars nowadays. I digress...

Strangely, it was only in recent years that you could order the Pendennis Club Cocktail at the club following the introduction of a drinks menu showcasing the various cocktails served at the bar over the last century. A recipe similar to this one is referenced in Charles H. Baker's *Gentleman's Companion* of 1946, though bizarrely an earlier citation from a supplement with the 1915 edition of Boothby's *World's Drinks and How to Mix Them* had the drink include dry vermouth in lieu of lime juice, and did not include bitters. While this makes a drink worth exploring, the superior variant is made with fresh lime juice and bitters; it is primarily tart with a flavor not too dissimilar to grapefruit, but also subtly sweet with a stoned fruit flavor throughout and a spicy, bracing finish from the bitters. A truly exceptional cocktail that deserves more acclaim.

PEGU CLUB

Unknown origin

2 OZ / 60 ML BEEFEATER GIN

¾ OZ / 22 ½ ML PIERRE FERRAND
ORANGE CURAÇAO

¾ OZ / 22 ½ ML FRESH LIME JUICE

1 DASH SCRAPPY'S CARDAMOM
BITTERS

1 DASH PEYCHAUD'S BITTERS

Add all the ingredients to a cocktail shaker, fill it with cubed ice, and shake hard for around 10 seconds. Strain into a pre-chilled cocktail glass and garnish with a wedge of fresh lime.

Another cocktail which surfaced from the old British colonies, the Pegu Club originates from Rangoon's gentleman's establishment of the same name. I have to admit the Pegu Club has never been a drink that sat right with me: having tried it with an array of different ingredients and again with various ratios, the balance always seemed off. The recipe from the 1930 *Savoy Cocktail Book*, for example, called for ⅔ gin to ⅓ Orange Curaçao, a teaspoon of lime juice, and a dash each of Peychaud's and Angostura Bitters. Whether it's a drink of its climate or the ingredients of the time, it wasn't until I started making subtle changes to the ingredients that it would come together. Slightly adjusting the ratio and replacing the warm spiced notes of Angostura with the Cardamom Bitters, introducing its herbal and citrus flavor profile, made every ingredient pop while maintaining the original beverage's style as a drier drink.

A BRIEF HISTORY

First opening its doors in 1871, the Pegu Club's membership rules stated it was open to *"All gentlemen interested in general society,"* although the truth is somewhat darker, with the local Burmese not welcome and widely treated as second-class citizens. After Britain lost Rangoon to Japan in the Second World War, the Japanese used the site as a brothel, putting the wheels in motion for its demise. Though the British would later regain control following the war and attempt to restore it to its former glories, Burma would gain independence from Great Britain in 1948, setting off a series of ongoing internal conflicts. Unfortunately, the building is now derelict and in a rapid state of decay. Those wishing to drink a Pegu Club in a modern-day Pegu Club may wish to head over to New York's SoHo district and pay a visit to the bar of that name opened in 2005 by Dale DeGroff pupil, Audrey Saunders.

JEREZ SOUR

Katie Nelson, The Columbia Room, Washington DC, USA

1 ½ oz / 45 ml BRANDY DE JEREZ

¾ oz / 22 ½ ml FRESH LEMON JUICE

¾ oz / 22 ½ ml ORGEAT SYRUP

1 DASH DR. ADAM ELMEGIRAB'S BOKER'S BITTERS

½ oz / 15 ml DRY OLOROSO SHERRY (FLOAT)

Add all the ingredients to a cocktail shaker, fill it with cubed ice, and shake hard for around 10 seconds. Strain into a pre-chilled cocktail glass and garnish with a speared twist of fresh orange zest and a cocktail cherry.

Even though it's historically relevant, and most importantly absolutely delicious, brandy has still to regain its rightful place in the world of cocktails, with it widely overlooked in favor of aged rums and whiskies. The impact of the Phylloxera bug, a louse that devastated vineyards in the mid-19th century, and both world wars in the early 20th century, should never be understated but many brandy companies have done little to embrace the modern drinker and shake off the image of stuffy, cigar smoke-filled, gentleman's clubs. On the flipside, it could be argued, a wider appreciation for the complex and intriguing flavors contained within brandies has still to be learned and its time in the sun is a matter not of if, but when...

Influenced by the Japanese Cocktail (*brandy, orgeat, lemon juice, and Boker's Bitters*), as found in Jerry Thomas's 1862 *Bartender's Manual*, the Jerez Sour was created by The Columbia Room bartender Katie Nelson after mulling over the suggestion by a chef to add crispy pig's head croquettes to their bar snack menu. Discussing its invention in an interview with Naren Young at the www.forkandshaker.com website, Nelson recalled *"What occurred to me was that I needed a drink with some tartness to cut through the fattiness of the croquette, but then also something with a richness and slight sweetness that would work with the rich toasted chestnut flavor in the dish. I decided to use brandy de Jerez with its sherry-enhanced flavor, as the base of a lemony sour sweetened with our house-made orgeat syrup, and given that sherry and almonds go so well together, top off with a float of sherry for aromatic impact. The delicate Boker's bitters really tie everything together and enhance the flavors."*

4. COCKTAILS

128

HEMINGWAY DAIQUIRI (AKA PAPA DOBLE)

*Constantino Ribalaigua Vert, La Floridita,
Havana, Cuba*

2 OZ / 60 ML HAVANA CLUB
3-YEAR-OLD RUM

⅓ OZ / 10 ML MARASCHINO
LIQUEUR

2 DASHES BITTERMENS
HOPPED GRAPEFRUIT
BITTERS

½ OZ / 15 ML FRESH PINK
GRAPEFRUIT JUICE

½ OZ / 15 ML FRESH LIME JUICE

½ OZ / 15 ML SUGAR SYRUP
(SEE PAGE 150)

*Add all the ingredients to a cocktail shaker, fill
it with cubed ice, and shake hard for around
10 seconds. Strain into a pre-chilled cocktail
glass and garnish with a wedge of fresh lime.*

To cover the life of Ernest Hemingway would in itself require a series of books, but his influence in the world of mixed drinks, from his own personal experiences often told through the beverages consumed by the characters in his books, cannot be overstated. Hemingway famously spent 1918–19 working for a Red Cross ambulance unit in Italy, where he was seriously injured by mortar fire; he returned to Europe in 1921 and lived in Paris from 1922–30, where he worked as a European correspondent for the *Toronto Daily Star*. In 1939, he moved to Cuba where he lived for 20 years. All these remarkable experiences put him front and center of some of the world's most influential cocktail capitals at a time of much social and political change.

A legendary imbiber who once stated, "*I drink to make other people more interesting,*" Hemingway spent much of his time propping up the bar at the famous Cuban haunt, El Floridita. While there, Hemingway would often chug back six of his Papa Dobles on a standard afternoon, throwing back 12 when he was really letting his hair down. The Papa Doble was a double Daiquiri created for Papa, as he was affectionately termed, comprising almost 4oz/120ml light rum, around a teaspoon of Maraschino liqueur, the juice of two whole limes, and again of half a grapefruit, all blended with ice. I've halved that recipe for reasons which really shouldn't need explaining, opted to shake it with ice, and added just a hint of Hopped Grapefruit Bitters to make it "*more interesting,*" as Hemingway would say. Though he sadly took his own life in 1961, you can still drink Hemingway Daiquiris at El Floridita next to a bronze statue of the great man leaning at the bar.

DR. COCKTAIL

Unknown origin

1 ½ oz / 45 ml APPLETON VX RUM

¾ oz / 22 ½ ml KRONAN SWEDISH PUNSCH

¾ oz / 22 ½ ml FRESH LIME JUICE

1 DASH BOB'S BITTERS ABBOTTS

Add all the ingredients to a cocktail shaker, fill it with cubed ice, and shake hard for around 10 seconds. Strain into a pre-chilled cocktail glass and garnish with a coin of fresh orange zest, snapped over the drink and then discarded.

Whereas the Daiquiri cocktail can be likened to The Beatles—arguably the most famous of their kind, loved the world over, and regularly enjoyed by all no matter their race, color, or creed—the Dr. Cocktail is more like Birmingham's heavy metal group Black Sabbath. Admittedly they both require a bit of getting used to, but there's a reason they have a cult following. The Dr. Cocktail is loud in liquid terms, but beneath the noise there's some undeniable beauty to be found.

Starting life in 1733 after the Swedish East India Company began importing red rice and sugarcane-based arrack (*see Aboukir Punch, page 102*) from Southeast Asia, Swedish Punsch originated as a made-to-order punch blending arrack with spices, rum, and sugar. This Punsch would later be bottled as an "RTD" (ready to drink), drawing comparisons with England's Pimm's if you must. The earliest book references to the Dr. Cocktail I could find are from Hugo Ensslin's 1916 *Recipes for Mixed Drinks* (1½oz/45ml Cederlund's Punch and juice of one lime), Harry MacElhone's 1927 *Barflies and Cocktails* (1oz/30ml each of Swedish Punsch, orange juice, and lemon juice), and Harry Craddock's 1930 *Savoy Cocktail Book* (2oz/60ml Swedish Punsch and 1oz/30ml lemon or lime juice)—all largely forgettable drinks if we're being honest. This adaptation is more complex than its original guise; it's rich, spicy, funky, and packed full of the hogo you expect to find in both Jamaican rum and Swedish Punsch, rounded off with the dry, spicy, oaked bitters.

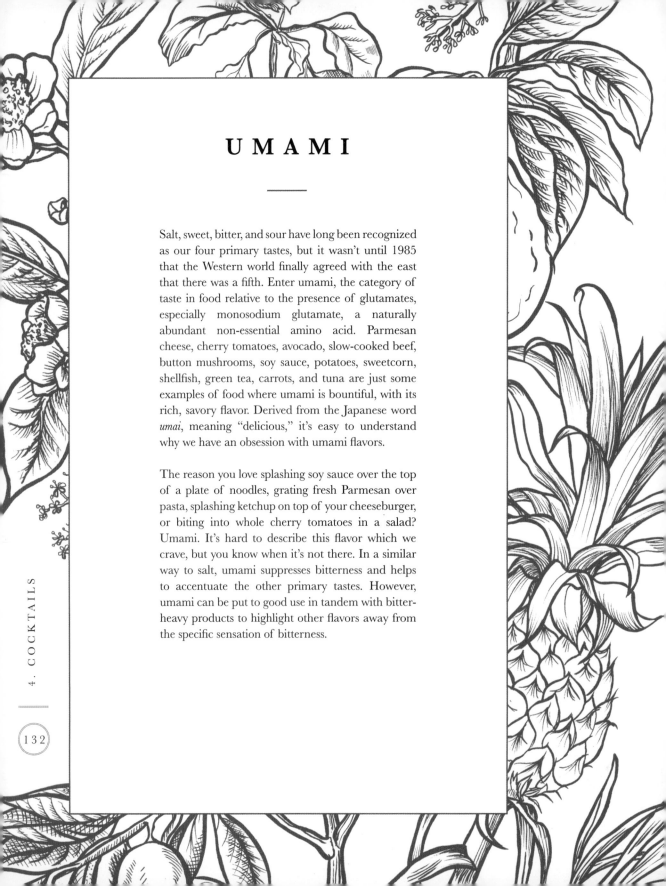

UMAMI

———

Salt, sweet, bitter, and sour have long been recognized as our four primary tastes, but it wasn't until 1985 that the Western world finally agreed with the east that there was a fifth. Enter umami, the category of taste in food relative to the presence of glutamates, especially monosodium glutamate, a naturally abundant non-essential amino acid. Parmesan cheese, cherry tomatoes, avocado, slow-cooked beef, button mushrooms, soy sauce, potatoes, sweetcorn, shellfish, green tea, carrots, and tuna are just some examples of food where umami is bountiful, with its rich, savory flavor. Derived from the Japanese word *umai*, meaning "delicious," it's easy to understand why we have an obsession with umami flavors.

The reason you love splashing soy sauce over the top of a plate of noodles, grating fresh Parmesan over pasta, splashing ketchup on top of your cheeseburger, or biting into whole cherry tomatoes in a salad? Umami. It's hard to describe this flavor which we crave, but you know when it's not there. In a similar way to salt, umami suppresses bitterness and helps to accentuate the other primary tastes. However, umami can be put to good use in tandem with bitter-heavy products to highlight other flavors away from the specific sensation of bitterness.

BLOODY MARY (IMPROVED)

Fernand Petiot, New York Bar, Paris, France

2 OZ / 60 ML KETEL ONE VODKA

4 OZ / 120 ML TOMATO JUICE

½ OZ / 15 ML FRESH LEMON JUICE

3 DASHES BITTER END
    MEMPHIS BARBECUE
    BITTERS

4 DASHES WORCESTERSHIRE
    SAUCE

2 DASHES TABASCO SAUCE

PINCH OF BLACK PEPPER

PINCH OF CELERY SALT

1 TEASPOON / 5 ML
    HORSERADISH OR
    ENGLISH MUSTARD

Add all the ingredients to a cocktail shaker, fill it with cubed ice, and place a strainer over the ice to hold it back before pouring into an empty cocktail shaker. Pour the liquid back into the iced shaker and repeat this process 4–5 times to chill and dilute. Pour the finished drink over fresh ice in a highball glass and garnish with a pickled onion and a grind of black pepper.

In a 1939 issue of *The New York Herald*, American author Lucius Beebe wrote: "*George Jessel's newest pick-me-up which is receiving attention from the town's paragraphers is called a Bloody Mary: half tomato juice, half vodka.*" So before we go any farther, that settles the argument as to who created the Bloody Mary. But what of Fernand Petiot's role in the creation of the drink? Quite simply, Petiot took Jessel's drink and embellished it, making it more like the drink we know and love. An improved Bloody Mary if you must. I actually refer to Jessel's original creation as the In-Flight Bloody Mary because I always order a vodka and tomato juice when flying (there's little chance they'll have additional seasoning on board to go full Petiot).

As with cups of tea, coffee, or more importantly in the case of this book, the Martini, the Bloody Mary is a very personal drink. Reassuringly, there's not much you can do to mess it up other than shaking it. Never shake it. Ever. Aerated tomato juice is not a good look. Simply start by combining vodka with good-quality tomato juice and then add flavorings as you see fit.

A RULE OF FIVES

A general rule of thumb from all the outstanding variants of the Bloody Mary I've tried is to incorporate ingredients that represent the five tastes. So for the drink above, the sour element is lemon juice, the sweet is tomato juice, the umami is Worcestershire sauce, the salt comes from the celery salt, and the bitter from the Memphis Barbecue Bitters.

CELERY SOUR

Jason Scott, Bramble, Edinburgh, Scotland

2 OZ / 60 ML MARTIN MILLER'S WESTBOURNE STRENGTH GIN

1 OZ / 30 ML FRESH LEMON JUICE

½ OZ / 15 ML FRESHLY PRESSED PINEAPPLE JUICE

½ OZ / 15 ML SUGAR SYRUP *(SEE PAGE 150)*

1 TEASPOON / 5 ML BITTER TRUTH CELERY BITTERS

½ OZ / 15 ML FRESH EGG WHITE

Add all the ingredients to a cocktail shaker, fill it with cubed ice, and shake hard for around 10 seconds. Strain into a pre-chilled coupe glass and garnish with a strip of celery peeled using a potato peeler.

You're probably wondering how on earth a drink called the Celery Sour has made its way into the umami section of this book, but I ask you to forget about the second part of the drink's name and concentrate on the first. Simply put, celery contains the amino acid glutamate, which is crucial to the taste of umami and the reason for its inclusion. Long favored by those trying to lose weight due to its low calorie content, celery stalks are very much a *love it* or *hate it* vegetable, which may put people off trying this drink, but note that celery stalks are not used in the production of celery bitters: celery seeds are king here. Profoundly vegetal, earthy, grassy, and lightly bitter, celery seeds are great with seafood, soups, and pickles, and they are now used widely by bartenders across the globe, thanks to the rediscovery of celery bitters.

Jason Scott's Celery Sour was one of the first cocktails containing Celery Bitters that I tried after they were released, and it still ranks as one of the best drinks I've ever encountered. The crisp, refreshing gin, the sharp citrus bite of the lemon, the tart sweetness of the fresh pineapple juice (please don't use the inferior concentrated variant), and the velvety, egg-white texture make for a tasty gin sour in its own right, but the addition of the bitters is magical, adding subtle hints of warm ginger, complex citrus, and the spiced vegetal notes from the celery seed. Don't let a dislike of celery make you overlook the drink—I've yet to come across one person who has not fallen in love with it.

OAXACA OLD FASHIONED

Phil Ward, Death & Co., New York City, USA

1 ½ OZ / 45 ML OCHO REPOSADO
   TEQUILA

½ OZ / 15 ML DEL MAGUEY SAN
   LUIS DEL RIO MEZCAL

2 DASHES BITTERMENS
   XOCOLATL MOLE BITTERS

1 TEASPOON / 5 ML AGAVE
   NECTAR

Add all the ingredients to a mixing vessel, fill it with cubed ice, and briskly stir for around 15–20 seconds. Strain into an ice-filled rocks glass and garnish with a coin of fresh orange zest snapped over and dropped into the drink.

Still largely misunderstood, mezcal is a Mexican spirit produced from any of 30 types of agave, a large fibrous plant often mistaken for a type of cactus. There are eight certified states in Mexico within mezcal's appellation of origin, although technically it can be produced anywhere in the country, with the state of Oaxaca being the largest producer. Mezcal gains its intense, complex flavor and predominant umami taste during the production process, with the agave plants cooked in pits dug into the ground ahead of the final fermentation and distillation stages. Tequila is technically a type of mezcal, but their production processes differ, and tequila can only be produced from blue agave.

If there is any drink that has opened up people's eyes to the potential of mezcal in mixed drinks, then this is it. Though many have dabbled with riffs on the Tequila Old Fashioned, this is the first drink I can recall seeing which combined the sweeter, drier, fruitier tequila with the complex leather, coffee, chili, smoke, vanilla, and spice of mezcals. The agave nectar adds just the right level of sweetness to round off the edges and intensify the flavors. The Mole Bitters will rarely find a better home, with the spicy cacao and cinnamon offering length to the drink.

ENGLISH MILK PUNCH

Davide Segat, Punch Room at The Edition Hotel, London, UK

1 FRESH PINEAPPLE

6 CLOVES

20 CORIANDER SEEDS

1 STICK OF CINNAMON

8 OZ / 240 ML FRESH LEMON JUICE

ZEST OF 2 LEMONS

1 LB / 450 G UNREFINED
   SUPERFINE / CASTER SUGAR

20 OZ / 600 ML PIERRE FERRAND
   1840 COGNAC (OR VSOP
   COGNAC)

10 OZ / 300 ML APPLETON ESTATE
   V/X RUM

10 OZ / 300 ML WOOD'S 100
   NAVY RUM

5 OZ / 150 ML BATAVIA ARRACK

1 OZ / 30 ML DR. ADAM
   ELMEGIRAB'S
   TEAPOT BITTERS

8 OZ / 240 ML STRONG GREEN TEA

40 OZ / 1.2 LITERS FRESHLY
   BOILED WATER

40 OZ / 1.2 LITERS HOT MILK

Peel and slice the pineapple into small chunks, then press with a rolling pin into the base of a vessel large enough to hold 6⅓ quarts/6 liters of liquid to extract all the juice. Grind the cloves, coriander seeds, and cinnamon stick, and add to the vessel.

Carefully grate the zest of two lemons, taking off as little pith as possible, then squeeze the lemons along with another four lemons to give you around 6oz/180ml of fresh lemon juice. Add this to the ground spices and pressed pineapple.

Add the sugar and stir until it has dissolved. Add the Cognac, rum, arrack, bitters, and tea, and stir thoroughly. Add the freshly boiled water, stir well, then cover and leave to macerate for no less than 6 hours.

After 6 hours, add the hot milk and squeeze another 2oz/60ml of fresh lemon juice, stir to combine, then allow to rest for 5 minutes or until the milk has curdled.

*Your punch now requires a two-step filtration. For the **first**, pour the liquid and solids through a fine-mesh sieve/strainer to extract large debris; repeat if necessary until all large debris has been removed. Allow to rest for a further 5 minutes and refrigerate if possible to allow the finer debris to rest at the base of your vessel.*

*For the **second** filtration, pour the liquid and fine sediment through a jelly bag to remove all the fine sediment. You may need to repeat this process until the liquid is clear.*

To finish, bottle the liquid in clean, sterilized* glass bottles and keep refrigerated. It should store for around a month in your fridge.

To serve, pour the punch over a large block of ice in a punch bowl garnished with seasonal fruits, berries, spices, and herbs. For individual serves, pour over ice in a small wine glass, tea cup, or goblet.

---

* To sterilize a bottle, wash the glass and lid in hot, soapy water and place upside-down in a 250°F/120°C/Gas ½ oven to dry for 30 minutes, then remove.

"*What's going on here?*" I hear you ask. Bromelain, an enzyme found in pineapple, breaks down casein, the proteins found in milk, leaving behind the texture and mouthfeel of milk but none of the color.

If just one person goes to the effort of making this punch, then my work here is done. Trust me, it's more than worth it. There's a reason it's gaining global popularity a few hundred years after it was originally created, no more so than at the Punch Room in London's Edition Hotel which probably serves the best adaptation of it that I've ever sampled in a bar. A truly remarkable beverage. Now go buy a jelly bag. You'll need it.

B . F . G

Author's own

1 ½ OZ / 45 ML DRAMBUIE

¾ OZ / 22 ½ ML COCCHI
VERMOUTH DI TORINO

⅓ OZ / 10 ML LAPHROAIG
10 YEAR OLD

2 DASHES DR. ADAM
ELMEGIRAB'S BOKER'S
BITTERS

Add all the ingredients to a mixing vessel, fill it with cubed ice, and briskly stir for around 15–20 seconds. Strain into a pre-chilled cocktail glass and garnish with a coin of fresh lemon zest snapped over and dropped into the drink.

This is another one of those hybrid drinks that just makes sense—this time a combination of two of the most famous Scotch whisky cocktails, the Rob Roy (*Scotch whisky, vermouth, bitters*) and the Rusty Nail (*Scotch whisky and Drambuie*). The name is a nod to the first recorded reference of a drink combining whisky and Drambuie, the B.I.F., from 1937, which was named for the British Industries Fair held annually in Birmingham from the 1920s until the mid-20th century.

I created this drink for the 2010 Drambuie Cocktail Competition. I formulated it specifically with the lead judge in mind—Simon Difford, of beverage industry publication *Difford's Guide*, after reading an article where he'd been looking for the perfect whisky for the Rusty Nail. His choice? Laphroaig 10 year old. A malt whisky from Islay with arguably the most complex flavor profile of any spirit in the world: rich, medicinal, citrus, vanilla, spice, meaty umami, iodine, black pepper, dark fruits… it just goes on and on, and is the perfect complement to the sweet, floral, medicinal Drambuie. The vermouth adds a drying acidity, thanks to the presence of wine, while the bitters add further length. The citrus flavors are prevalent and are highlighted by the fresh, aromatic garnish.

MAYAS DAIQUIRI

David Cordoba, Bramble, Edinburgh, Scotland

½ FRESH RIPE AVOCADO

2 OZ / 60 ML BACARDI OCHO

1 DASH SCRAPPY'S CARDAMOM
    BITTERS

½ OZ / 15 ML FRESH LIME JUICE

¾ OZ / 22 ½ ML AGAVE SYRUP

Peel and chop the avocado, then add it to the base of a cocktail shaker and muddle into a purée. Add the remaining ingredients, stir to combine, then fill with cubed ice and shake hard for around 10 seconds. Strain into a pre-chilled coupe glass and garnish with a pineapple frond.

Writing this in early 2017 the world is in the midst of a crisis, and no, it's not anything to do with Donald Trump. There's a world shortage of avocados. The fruit of the avocado tree has quickly gone from a luxury item to an absolute essential, with consumption in America alone increasing more than three-fold; the average US citizen is now eating 5lbs (2¼kg) per year versus the 1½lbs (⅔kg) consumed in 1990. The proliferation of Mexican-influenced food is undoubtedly a factor, but there is also the fact that an increasingly health-conscious world has switched on to the healthy fats contained within avocado which make it an ideal substitute for the likes of butter. Avocado's umami taste is also likely a factor in our growing obsession.

The cocktail world has seen a small uptake of drinks which utilize the fruit, typically in Bloody Mary variants and blended Margaritas, though the Mayas Daiquiri is the king of them all. Influenced by an avocado and sugar purée his grandmother used to treat him to, Cordoba would take the classic Daiquiri (*rum, lime, sugar*) and add his own twist, using an aged rum that features pronounced notes of coffee, chocolate, toffee, and caramel; these flavors all partner wonderfully with avocado, in lieu of the drier light rum traditionally used in Daiquiris. The recipe also swaps out sugar for the honey-like agave nectar, while fresh lime juice provides balance and my addition of Cardamom Bitters adds further length and depth. To get the right consistency after shaking, ensure you use wetter ice, or add a touch of water if you're pulling ice straight from the freezer.

ADONIS COCKTAIL

Unknown, Waldorf-Astoria Hotel, New York City, USA

1 ½ oz / 45 ml DRY OLOROSO SHERRY

1 ½ oz / 45 ml COCCHI VERMOUTH DI TORINO

2 DASHES REGANS' ORANGE BITTERS NO. 6

Add all the ingredients to your mixing vessel, fill it with cubed ice, and briskly stir for around 15–20 seconds. Strain into a pre-chilled cocktail glass and garnish with a slice of orange cut into a quarter, rubbed around the rim of the glass, then dropped into the drink.

There was a time when any major event would be honored with the creation of a cocktail, such as the Moonwalk created by the Savoy's Joe Gilmore to commemorate the Apollo 11 moon landing, or the Rob Roy, which was formulated to honor the premiere of the operetta which shares its name. The Adonis was similarly created in the 1880s, and named for the first Broadway musical to run for 500 performances.

Not too dissimilar to the makeup of the Martini (*gin, vermouth, bitters*), the Adonis is an old-timey, aromatic cocktail which is great before or after dinner, and especially so as an accompaniment to a cheeseboard. The base spirit of Oloroso sherry is big on umami, with a dried-fruit, spice, and leather flavor profile, and it perfectly complements the dark fruits and berries in the sweet vermouth. The Adonis is the sweeter of the *Jekyll & Hyde* cocktails, the other being the Bamboo that follows, and favors spicier, vegetal orange bitters to complement the nutty sherry and fruity vermouth. Look no farther than Regans' Orange Bitters No. 6, although if a sweeter orange profile is desired, Angostura Orange Bitters will do the trick.

144

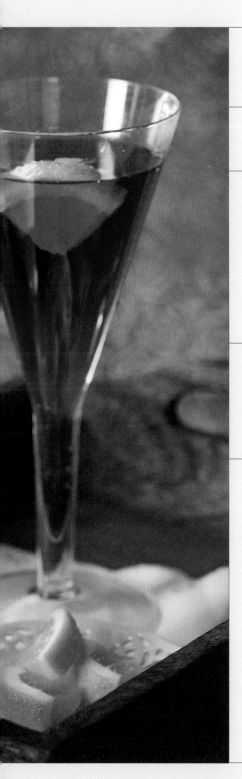

BAMBOO

Louis Eppinger, Grand Hotel, Yokohama, Japan

1 ½ OZ / 45 ML FINO SHERRY

1 ½ OZ / 45 ML NOILLY PRAT VERMOUTH

1 DASH ANGOSTURA ORANGE BITTERS

1 DASH AROMATIC BITTERS *(ANGOSTURA, BITTER TRUTH OLD TIME, OR DR. ADAM ELMEGIRAB'S ORINOCO AROMATIC BITTERS)*

Add all the ingredients to a mixing vessel, fill it with cubed ice, and briskly stir for around 15–20 seconds. Strain into a pre-chilled cocktail glass and garnish with a slice of lemon cut into a quarter, rubbed around the rim of the glass, then dropped into the drink.

When dry vermouth first became widely available in the late 19th and early 20th centuries, the proliferation of dry vermouth cocktails that followed would typically mimic their sweet cousins; the Martini led to the Dry Martini and the Adonis spawned the Bamboo. The latter, created in Yokohama by German-born bartender Louis Eppinger, would gain popularity at a time when Japan was largely embracing international drinks' ideology.

Turning the Adonis on its head by replacing the nutty, spicy Oloroso sherry and sweet, fruity vermouth, Eppinger would employ the dry, acidic Fino sherry and the soft fruit, crisp, and floral notes from the dry vermouth. To lend balance and length I suggest reaching for an orange bitters that leans toward a sweeter, candied-orange profile, in tandem with the spiced aromatic bitters, though other fruit bitters are worth experimenting with, namely lemon, cucumber, peach, or Spanish.

AUTUMN NEGRONI

Danny Whelan, Kelvingrove Cafe,
Glasgow, Scotland

1 oz / 30 ML THE BOTANIST GIN

1 oz / 30 ML CAMPARI

1 oz / 30 ML COCCHI VERMOUTH
    DI TORINO INFUSED WITH
    PORCINI MUSHROOM
    (SEE PAGE 154)

1 DASH BOB'S CORIANDER
    BITTERS

Add all the ingredients to a mixing vessel, fill
it with cubed ice, and briskly stir for around
15–20 seconds. Strain into an ice-filled rocks
glass and garnish with a dried lemon wheel.

As far as foolproof recipes go, the Negroni has them all beat. It's fair to say I've never had a Negroni I didn't enjoy, and it's one of the few cocktails you can order in virtually any bar in the world. Even in the worst dive bar or most horribly, unkempt pub, there's a good chance they'll have a dusty bottle of Campari and vermouth lurking behind the bar. Order three shots of gin, vermouth, and Campari, ask for a glass of ice, and you've got all you need. Of course it can be argued that the ratio can be adjusted, or you may even wish to replace gin with (i) Prosecco for a Negroni Sbagliato, (ii) soda for an Americano, (iii) rye for an Old Pal, (iv) bourbon for a Boulevardier, (v) rum for a Bencini, or (vi) tequila for a Rosita, but each are wonderful in their own right, and incredibly easy to make.

For foods which fully epitomize this chapter, mushroom takes some beating, with all variants containing umami. Darker mushrooms contain more than lighter ones, and cooked mushrooms more than raw, though in this case, the same principle applies to dried mushrooms as with fresh. Infusing the sweet vermouth with dried porcini mushrooms adds an incredible earthy, woody, and nutty character, which is wonderful with the spicy, bitter orange Campari, the dry, fresh gin, and the warm, lemony-citrus coriander bitters, which round things off.

HONG KONG BRUNCH

Patrick Noir, M.V.P., Dublin, Ireland

1 oz / 30 ml BEEFEATER 24 GIN

1 oz / 30 ml PIERRE FERRAND
1840 COGNAC (OR VSOP
COGNAC)

¾ oz / 22 ½ ml FRESHLY PRESSED
PINEAPPLE JUICE

⅓ oz / 10 ml FRESH LIME JUICE

⅓ oz / 10 ml LAPSANG SOUCHONG
SYRUP *(SEE PAGE 152)*

1 DASH ABSINTHE

2 DASHES PEYCHAUD'S
BITTERS

Add all the ingredients to a cocktail shaker, fill it with cubed ice, and shake hard for around 10 seconds. Strain into an ice-filled highball glass and garnish with a pineapple frond.

Drinks that contain more than one base spirit are still largely ignored, probably because of the unwritten rules surrounding the creation of cocktails, but when you learn and understand the reasons why a sole base spirit is preferable, it makes it easier to break the rule and find ways to blend two spirits or more. Dark rum and brandy have long been partnered in mixed drinks such as the English Milk Punch *(see page 138)*, gin and light rum in the likes of the Maiden's Prayer (also including Cointreau and lemon juice), or bourbon and Cognac in the Vieux Carré, but gin (unexpectedly) achieves great things combined with funky Jamaican rum and, in the case of M.V.P.'s Hong Kong Brunch, with Cognac too.

Much like Laphroaig and mezcal, Lapsang Souchong tea isn't for everyone with its smoky umami-rich flavors, but it's an oddly refreshing cup and very, very moreish. When I first sampled the tea I wasn't a fan but I've been drawn back to it over the years, and was pleasantly surprised at the way it was utilized in this drink when I had the opportunity to taste it on a trip to Dublin. Even now when I look at the recipe it doesn't make sense, but it's not until you remove the associated names and focus on the flavors contained within that it all comes together; the fresh, orange-heavy gin pairs wonderfully with the stoned-fruit flavor of the Cognac, the tart refreshing aspect of pineapple and lime juices works in harmony with the tea syrup, and the herbaceous, spiced absinthe and bitters add backbone with hints of licorice and anise.

KEY INGREDIENT RECIPES

——

What follows is a guide to making the various syrups, infusions, and tinctures outlined in the cocktail recipes section, each being crucial to the specific recipe they are utilized.

DEMERARA SUGAR SYRUP

——

20oz/600g Demerara sugar
10oz/300ml water

Combine sugar and water in a suitable mixing vessel and stir vigorously until the sugar has fully dissolved. Using a funnel, pour into clean, sterilized glass bottles (*see page 139*), then seal, label, and refrigerate. It keeps for up to 4 weeks.
TIP: If using granulated sugar, you can speed up the process of dissolving by grinding the sugar to a finer powder using a food processor.

SUGAR SYRUP

——

20oz/600g unrefined cane sugar
10oz/300ml water

Combine the sugar and water in a suitable mixing vessel and stir vigorously until the sugar has fully dissolved. Using a funnel, pour into clean, sterilized glass bottles (*see page 139*), then seal, label, and refrigerate. It will keep for up to 4 weeks.
TIP: If using granulated sugar you can speed up the process of dissolving by grinding the sugar to a finer powder using a food processor.

VANILLA SUGAR SYRUP

1 vanilla bean/pod
20oz/600g unrefined cane sugar
10oz/300ml water

Score the vanilla bean/pod and add to the sugar, agitate thoroughly and allow to rest for at least 1 week before using. Combine the vanilla-infused sugar and water in a suitable mixing vessel and stir vigorously until the sugar has fully dissolved. Using a funnel, pour into clean, sterilized glass bottles (*see page 139*), then seal, label, and refrigerate. It will keep for up to 4 weeks.

TIP: If using granulated sugar you can speed up the process of dissolving by grinding the sugar to a finer powder using a food processor.

PINEAPPLE SYRUP

1 pineapple
20oz/600g unrefined cane sugar
10oz/300ml water

Peel the pineapple and cut it into cubes. Using a citrus press, squeeze the pineapple cubes to extract all juice, also adding the squeezed pulp. Combine with the sugar and water in a suitable mixing vessel and stir vigorously until the sugar has fully dissolved. Allow to rest for 24 hours then strain through a fine-mesh strainer. Using a funnel, pour into clean, sterilized glass bottles (*see page 139*), then seal, label, and refrigerate. It will keep for up to 4 weeks.

TIP: If using granulated sugar you can speed up the process of dissolving by grinding the sugar to a finer powder using a food processor.

GUNPOWDER
TEA SYRUP

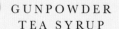

*⅔oz/20ml Gunpowder
Tea Tincture (as right)
22½oz/680ml Sugar
Syrup (see page 150)*

Combine the tincture and syrup in a suitable mixing vessel and stir until fully combined. Using a funnel, pour into clean, sterilized glass bottles (*see page 139*), then seal, label, and refrigerate. It will keep for up to 4 weeks.

GUNPOWDER
TEA TINCTURE

*1oz/30g gunpowder tea
5oz/150ml 96% ABV
neutral spirit
5oz/150ml water*

Combine both the tea and spirit in a clean jar, stir thoroughly, and allow to rest for 2 days. Strain through coffee filter paper, then add the water. Using a funnel, pour into a clean, sterilized dasher bottle (*see page 139*). It will keep indefinitely and has an ABV of approximately 45–48%.

LAPSANG SOUCHONG SYRUP

*20oz/600g unrefined cane sugar
10oz/300ml strong brewed Lapsang Souchong tea*

Combine the sugar and tea in a suitable mixing vessel and stir vigorously until the sugar has fully dissolved. Using a funnel, pour into clean, sterilized glass bottles (*see page 139*), then seal, label, and refrigerate. It will keep for up to 4 weeks.

TIP: If using granulated sugar you can speed up the process of dissolving by grinding the sugar to a finer powder using a food processor.

MACE TINCTURE

1oz/30g freshly ground mace blades
5oz/150ml 96% ABV neutral spirit
5oz/150 ml water

Combine both the mace and spirit in a clean jar, stir thoroughly, and allow to rest for 5 days. Strain through coffee filter paper, then add the water. Using a funnel, pour into a clean, sterilized dasher bottle (*see page 139*). It will keep indefinitely and has an ABV of approximately 45–48%.

LEMON SHERBET

Zest of 6 lemons
20oz/600g unrefined
cane sugar
18oz/540ml fresh
lemon juice

Using a vegetable peeler remove the zest from the lemon, leaving behind as much pith as possible, and combine with the sugar. Agitate thoroughly with your hands to ensure the oils of the zest and sugar have fully integrated and rest for 24 hours. Add the fresh lemon juice and stir until dissolved. Strain through a fine-mesh sieve/strainer, then funnel into a clean, sterilized glass bottle (*see page 139*) and refrigerate. It will keep for 3 days.

GRAPEFRUIT & CARDAMOM SHERBET

Zest of 3 ruby grapefruits
4 green cardamom pods
20oz/600g unrefined cane sugar
9oz/270ml fresh ruby grapefruit juice
9oz/270ml fresh lemon juice

Using a vegetable peeler remove the zest from the grapefruit, leaving behind as much pith as possible, and combine with the sugar along with crushed cardamom pods. Agitate thoroughly with your hands to ensure the oils of the zest, cardamom, and sugar have fully integrated and rest for 24 hours. Add the fresh grapefruit and lemon juice, and stir until dissolved. Strain through a fine-mesh sieve/strainer, then funnel into a clean, sterilized glass bottle (*see page 139*) and refrigerate. It will keep for 3 days.

PORCINI-INFUSED VERMOUTH

½oz/15g dried porcini mushrooms
23oz/700ml Cocchi Vermouth di Torino

Roughly chop the mushrooms, then combine them with the vermouth in a clean, sterilized glass jar (*see page 139*), stir thoroughly, and allow to rest for 2 weeks, agitating daily. Strain through coffee filter paper, then, using a funnel, pour back into the empty vermouth bottle, seal, label, and refrigerate. It will keep for 4 weeks.

JASMINE TEA-INFUSED VODKA

1 jasmine tea bag
23oz/700ml Ketel One Vodka

Combine both the tea and spirit in a clean, sterilized glass jar (*see page 139*), stir thoroughly, and allow to rest for 30 minutes. Remove the teabag and squeeze to extract all liquid. Using a funnel, pour back into the empty vodka bottle, seal, and label. It will keep indefinitely.

PANDAN-INFUSED TAWNY PORT

8 pandan leaves
23oz/700ml Tawny port

Roughly chop the pandan leaves, then combine with the port in a clean, sterilized glass jar (*see page 139*). Stir thoroughly and allow to rest for 1 week, agitating daily. Strain through coffee filter paper, then, using a funnel, pour back into the empty port bottle, seal, label, and refrigerate. It will keep for 4 weeks.

KOSHER SALT, CELERY SALT, & SUGAR MIX

1oz/30g Kosher salt
1oz/30g celery salt
*1oz/30g unrefined
cane sugar*

Combine all the ingredients and mix thoroughly. Store in a clean, sterilized glass jar (*see page 139*) in a cool, dry place. It will keep indefinitely.

VANILLA SALT

1 vanilla bean/pod
8oz/240g table salt

Score the vanilla bean/pod and add to the salt, agitate thoroughly, and allow to rest for at least 1 week before using. Store in a cool, dry place. It will keep indefinitely.

SALINE SOLUTION

1oz/30g table salt
10oz/300ml water

Combine the salt and water in a suitable mixing vessel and stir vigorously until the salt has dissolved. Using a funnel, pour into a clean, sterilized dasher bottle (*see page 139*). It will keep indefinitely.

BITTERS GLOSSARY

The following is a concise snapshot of all the bitters featured in the cocktail recipes section. This glossary identifies the key botanicals and flavorings associated with each bitters and can be used to determine the specific tastes they offer, while providing an idea of what to use as a substitute should the original bottling be unavailable.

AMARGO CHUNCHO BITTERS
(Peru – 40% ABV):
Baking spices, bittersweet, aromatic

ANGOSTURA AROMATIC BITTERS
(Trinidad & Tobago – 44.7% ABV):
Warm spice, cherry, cola

ANGOSTURA ORANGE BITTERS
(Trinidad & Tobago – 28% ABV):
Candied orange, spice, coriander

BITTER END MEMPHIS BARBECUE BITTERS
(USA – 45% ABV):
Smoke, chipotle, spice

BITTER TRUTH CELERY BITTERS
(Germany – 44% ABV):
Celery, lemongrass, ginger

BITTER TRUTH OLD TIME BITTERS
(Germany – 39% ABV):
Clove, gingerbread, cardamom

BITTERMENS HOPPED GRAPEFRUIT BITTERS
(USA – 53% ABV):
Bitter grapefruit, pine, citrus

BITTERMENS XOCOLATL MOLE BITTERS
(USA – 53% ABV):
Bitter chocolate, black pepper, rich

BOB'S ABBOTTS BITTERS
(England – 41.8% ABV):
Herbal, spicy, bitter

BOB'S CORIANDER BITTERS
(England – 30% ABV):
Vegetal, coriander, bittersweet

DALE DEGROFF'S PIMENTO BITTERS
(France – 45% ABV):
Clove, licorice, warm spices

DR. ADAM ELMEGIRAB'S APHRODITE BITTERS
(Scotland – 38% ABV):
Cacao, coffee, chili

DR. ADAM ELMEGIRAB'S BOKER'S BITTERS
(Scotland – 31.5% ABV):
Cardamom, citrus, bitter coffee

DR. ADAM ELMEGIRAB'S DANDELION & BURDOCK BITTERS
(Scotland – 42% ABV):
Licorice, spice, earthy

DR. ADAM ELMEGIRAB'S ORINOCO AROMATIC BITTERS
(Scotland – 45% ABV):
Baking spice, bittersweet, molasses

DR. ADAM ELMEGIRAB'S SPANISH BITTERS
(Scotland – 38% ABV):
Floral, citrus, marmalade

DR. ADAM ELMEGIRAB'S TEAPOT BITTERS
(Scotland – 38% ABV):
Black tea, vanilla, baking spice

PEYCHAUD'S BITTERS
(USA – 35% ABV):
Anise, spice, stoned fruit

REGANS' ORANGE NO. 6 BITTERS
(USA – 45% ABV):
Bitter orange, cardamom, spice

SCRAPPY'S CARDAMOM BITTERS
(USA – 52% ABV):
Sweet, cardamom, citrus

INDEX

Aboukir Punch 102
absinthe 30, 31, 44
  Bijou 71
  Hong Kong Brunch 149
  Sazerac 78
  Tuxedo 84
Adonis Cocktail 144
Akhavan, Joseph 102
Akvavit
  Nordic Club 87
alcoholic strength 26, 28, 32
Amargo Bitters 11, 22
Amaro Montenegro
  Ol' Dirty Bastard 74
Añejo Highball 88
angelica root 13, 42
Angostura bark 17, 41
Angostura Bitters 10, 11, 20,
  22, 23, 30, 42, 49
  Angostura myth 16, 17
Anisette
  Montana 101
apricot brandy
  Pendennis Club Cocktail
  124
Army & Navy 116
aroma 38
arrack
  English Milk Punch
  138–139
Autumn Negroni 146

Baker, Charles H. 23, 69,
  110, 124
Bamboo 145
bartending equipment 52–53
beer cocktails
  A Beer and a Smoke 109
  Porter Sangaree 73
B.F.G. 140
Bijou 71
The Bitter Truth 10, 23,
  25, 27
bittering agents see
  botanicals
Bittermens 10, 24, 25, 27,
  43, 49
bitterness 10, 11, 30, 39, 48
  appreciation of 14
  cocktails 58–85
  negative associations 14
bitters
  alcoholic strength 26,
  28, 32
  defining 10–11
  glossary 156–157
  history of 10, 12–13,

20–25
  manufacturing process
  26–33
  medicinal uses 9, 10,
  12–13, 20–21
  selecting and pairing
  48–49
  sub-categories 10
Bloody Mary 38, 133
Bloody Mary (Improved) 133
Bob's Bitters 23
Boker's Bitters 9, 11, 21,
  24, 43
Bolognese, Valentino 69
The Bon Vivant's
  Companion or How
  to Mix Drinks (Jerry
  Thomas) 8, 67, 69
botanicals 10, 11, 13, 26, 29,
  40–47
  bittering agents 29, 41–47
  definition 40
  distillation 30–31
  extraction 30–31
  fresh/dried 29
  maceration 26, 30
  percolation 30
  primary flavorings 29
  safety 26, 28
  tinctures 28, 30
bourbon
  Old Fashioned 66
Bradsell, Dick 94
The Bramble 94
brandy
  Jerez Sour 128
  Trinidad Especial 69
  see also apricot brandy;
  Cognac
Brandy Crusta 61
Broom, Liam 123

Campari
  Autumn Negroni 146
Celery Gimlet 113
Celery Sour 134
Champagne Cocktail 97
Chartreuse
  Bijou 71
  Celery Gimlet 113
Chelsea Dove 105
cinchona bark 11, 16, 28, 41
citrus fruits 45, 114
The Clover 87
Cocchi Americano
  Downriver 123
cocktails

bartending equipment
  52–53
  glassware 38, 39, 54
  history of 15
  preparation 55–56
  see also individual index
  entries
Cognac
  Brandy Crusta 61
  Champagne Cocktail 97
  East India Cocktail 98
  English Milk Punch
  138–139
  Hong Kong Brunch 149
  Sazerac 78
Coleman, Ada 103
Conigliaro, Tony 70
Cooper, Rob 101
Cordoba, David 143
Corn & Oil 59
Curaçao
  Añejo Highball 88
  Brandy Crusta 61
  East India Cocktail 98
  Martinez/Manhattan 62
  Pegu Club 127
Cynar
  Ol' Dirty Bastard 74

Daiquiri 104, 130, 143
dandelion root 11, 42
Dark 'N' Stormy 88
DeGroff, Dale 88
digestifs 10, 58
Downriver 123
Dr. Adam Elmegirab's
  Bitters 9, 10, 24–25,
  32–33, 49
Dr. Cocktail 131
Drambuie
  B.F.G. 140
  Fosbury Flip 91
Dry Martini 49, 63, 77

East India Cocktail 98
elderflower liqueur 101
  Celery Gimlet 113
Embury, David A. 116
English Milk Punch 138–139
Eppinger, Louis 145
ethanol 12, 28

Falernum
  Corn & Oil 59
  Queen's Park Special 81
Fee Brothers 20, 23, 28
Fernet Branca

Flintlock 70
  Hanky Spanky 103
Flintlock 70
Florabotanica 92
Forbes, Jack 103
Fosbury, Dick 91
Fosbury Flip 91
Fougner, G. Selmer 116

gentian root 11, 16, 30–31,
  42
Gimlet 113
gin
  Army & Navy 116
  Autumn Negroni 146
  Bijou 71
  Celery Gimlet 113
  Celery Sour 134
  Chelsea Dove 105
  Dry Martini 63, 77
  Flintlock 70
  Florabotanica 92
  Gin Pahit 82
  Gin Piaj 82
  Hanky Spanky 103
  Hong Kong Brunch 149
  London Calling 115
  Manhattan 62
  Nordic Club 87
  Pegu Club 127
  Pendennis Club Cocktail
  124
  Tuxedo 84
  see also sloe gin
glassware 38, 39, 54
  chilling 55
  sugar or salt rims 55
glycerin 11, 23, 28
Gonzalez, Giuseppe 69
Grand Marnier
  Brandy Crusta 61
Grog 113

Hanky Spanky 103
Harvard 63
Hawtrey, Charles 103
Hemingway, Ernest 97, 110,
  130
Hemingway Daiquiri 130
herbs and flowers 46
Hippocrates 12, 13
Hong Kong Brunch 149
hops 11, 14, 43

infusions
  jasmine tea-infused vodka
  154

pandan-infused tawny port
  102, 155
porcini-infused vermouth
  154

Jepson, Chris 115
Jerez Sour 128
Jessel, George 133
Johnson, Harry 71, 98, 99,
  101

Kangaroo 63
Kennedy Manhattan 64
Khoosh Bitters 20

La Paloma 105
Lady Colombia 106
Lambert, Paul 59
lassi 118, 119
Lawrence, Alex 106
London Calling 115
Long Vodka 16

Macchu Pisco
  Pisco Sour 120
  Trinidad Especial 69
MacElhone, Harry 84, 131
McGarry, Jack 73
Manhattan 49, 62, 63, 64
manufacturing process
  26–33
  bespoke bottlings 25
  botanicals see botanicals
  compounder's licence 27
  filtration 31–33
  fining technique 32
  legal issues 27
  non-alcoholic bitters 28
  solvents 28, 30
Maraschino
  East India Cocktail 98
  Florabotanica 92
  Hemingway Daiquiri 130
  Martinez/Manhattan 62
  Tuxedo 84
Martinez 62
Mayas Daiquiri 143
Meehan, Jim 109
Mexican "Firing Squad"
  Special 110
Mezcal
  A Beer and a Smoke 109
  Oaxaca Old Fashioned
  137
Michelada 109
Montana 101
Moonwalk 144
Morris, Victor 120

Negroni 104, 146
Nelson, Katie 128

Noir, Patrick 149
Nordic Club 87

Oaxaca Old Fashioned 137
Ol' Dirty Bastard 74
Old Fashioned 15, 66, 67,
  124
orange bitters 11, 23, 49

Palmetto 63
Papa Doble 130
Pegu Club 127
Pendennis Club Cocktail 124
Petiot, Fernand 133
Peychaud's 10, 11, 20, 23
Pink Gin 82
Pisco Sour 120
port
  Aboukir Punch 102
  pandan-infused tawny port
  102, 155
Porter Sangaree 73
Prohibition 21–22, 116
punches 102

quassia bark 11, 43
Queen's Park Special 81
Queen's Park Swizzle 81
quinine 13, 41

Regans' Orange Bitters
  23, 49
rhubarb root 43
Ribalaigua Vert,
  Constantino 130
Rob Roy 63, 140, 144
rum 107
  Aboukir Punch 102
  Añejo Highball 88
  Corn & Oil 59
  Dr. Cocktail 131
  English Milk Punch
  138–139
  Fosbury Flip 91
  Hemingway Daiquiri 130
  Kennedy Manhattan 64
  Lady Colombia 106
  Mayas Daiquiri 143
  Queen's Park Special 81
  Treacle 94
Russian Spring Punch 94
Rusty Nail 140
Rye Manhattan 49
rye whiskey
  Martinez 62

saline solution 104, 114, 155
salt mixes
  Kosher salt, celery salt &
  sugar mix 155
  vanilla salt 155

saltiness 39, 48
  cocktails 104–113
Sangaree 73
Santina, Joseph 61
Sazerac 78
Scott, Jason 134
Scrappy's Bitters 24
Segat, Davide 138
sensory responses 38–39
shaken cocktails 55–56
sherbets
  grapefruit & cardamom
  sherbet 154
  lemon sherbet 153
sherry
  Adonis Cocktail 144
  Bamboo 145
  Jerez Sour 128
  London Calling 115
  Ol' Dirty Bastard 74
Shira, Bar 74
Shrubs 43
Siegert, Dr. J.G.B. 12, 16, 82
sloe gin
  Montana 101
sounds, and their effects on
  taste 39
sourness 39, 48
  cocktails 114–131
spices 47
stirred cocktails 55
Stoughton, Richard 12–13
Suze 30–31
Swedish Punsch 131
sweetness 39, 48
  cocktails 86–103
swizzled cocktails 56
Sydenham's Bitters 13
syrups
  Demerera sugar syrup 150
  gunpowder tea syrup 70,
  152
  Lapsang Souchong syrup
  149, 152
  pineapple syrup 151
  sugar syrup 150
  vanilla sugar syrup 151

taste and flavor 57
  science of 36–39
  taste buds 38
  see also bitterness;
  saltiness; sourness;
  sweetness; umami
temperance movement 21
tequila
  Mexican "Firing Squad"
  Special 110
  Oaxaca Old Fashioned
  137
Thomas, Jerry 8, 67, 69

thrown cocktails 56
tincture-style bitters 24
tinctures 11, 28, 30
  gunpowder tea tincture
  152
  mace tincture 153
tonka bean 26, 28
Treacle 94
Trinidad Especial 69
Trinidad Sour 69
Turf 63
Tuxedo 84

umami 39, 48
  cocktails 132–149
Underberg 11

Van Ark, Carroll 116
Vanilla & Coconut Lassi 118
vermouth 12
  Adonis Cocktail 144
  Autumn Negroni 146
  Bamboo 145
  B.F.G. 140
  Bijou 71
  Dry Martini 63, 77
  Hanky Spanky 103
  Kennedy Manhattan 64
  Lady Colombia 106
  Martinez/Manhattan 62
  Montana 101
  Ol' Dirty Bastard 74
  porcini-infused vermouth
  146, 154
  Tuxedo 84
Vermouth Cocktail family 63
visual appeal 38
vodka
  Bloody Mary (Improved)
  133
  Downriver 123
  jasmine tea-infused vodka
  154
  Vanilla & Coconut Lassi
  118

Ward, Phil 137
Whelan, Danny 146
whisky
  B.F.G. 140
  see also bourbon; rye
  whiskey
wild cherry bark 44
Williams, Jason 92
wormwood 11, 12, 13, 16,
  30, 44
Wrangel, Carl 64

Young, Naren 113

INDEX

159

ACKNOWLEDGEMENTS

———

Though it'll be my name on the front of this work and receiving full credit as the author, books are a collaborative effort, with content derived from a lifetime of lessons and experiences. Quite simply, I couldn't have done this on my own and there are so many people who deserve some form of recognition, more than will be mentioned below.

First of all, a huge thank you to my mum for encouraging me as a child to eat and cook a wide variety of foods, for generally just being an amazing woman, and for indirectly driving on my stubborn self by always asking when I was going to get a real job once I started bartending.

Claire Scott, the first head bartender I worked under, for being largely responsible for setting me on the right path when I started working on bars and for showing me a career could be made behind the pine.

The Ahmed family, John Jones, Barrie Brown, and numerous others who gave me creative freedom with their businesses under my previous guise while consulting and bartending as Evo-lution. Without those years I wouldn't have been able to expand my knowledge and skills, especially as I entered the world of business on my own.

Though we've never directly worked together, the careers, determination, and successes of Mike Aikman and Jason Scott from Bramble in Edinburgh were always an inspiration to a bartender from Aberdeen looking to find his way in the world and gain wider recognition. I hope I've repaid that inspiration in some way as they now enter the world of spirits manufacture.

The Bitter Truth's Stephan Berg & Alexander Hauck, as well as Janet & Avery Glasser of Bittermens, for offering support, encouragement, and advice when I set off starting my own spirits production business.

Dave Wondrich for setting a new standard in drinks writing and research, and in how to reach a conclusion when attempting to unravel the hazy history of spirits and cocktails. Thanks for always being there whenever I had a query.

My commissioning editor, Pete Jorgensen, for having the patience of a saint while I reimagined, rejigged, researched, and rewrote much of the original ideas and content we devised.

The bartenders of Dusk and Orchid in my hometown of Aberdeen, for always keeping my Martinez glass topped up over the years and throughout the many late nights writing this book. My caffeine and coconut-water consumption always seems to increase the day after I visit them as well, not 100 percent sure why?

Abigail, Kim, Terry, and Nathan for the design, artwork, imagery, and editing, as well as the team at RPS for making my vision for the book a reality.

And last, but not in no way least, I want to give special mention to the one person who has to deal with me on a daily basis. At the time I started writing she was my fiancée, but as I sign off this last page I'm delighted to now call her my wife. Steffie, thank you for always being there, encouraging, supporting, and giving me the drive to do what I do.